CROWN OF THE WORLD
A View of the Inner Arctic

CROWN
OF THE WORLD
A View of the Inner Arctic

✦✦

CORA CHENEY AND BEN PARTRIDGE
Illustrated with photographs and maps

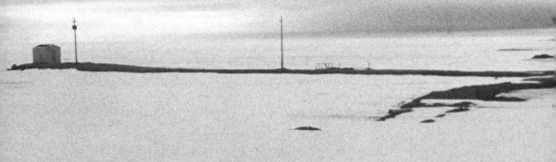

DODD, MEAD & COMPANY • NEW YORK

PHOTOGRAPHS COURTESY OF:
An Exxon Photo, 106
National Portrait Gallery, London, 17 *left*
Naval Photographic Center, 53, 92, 93, 107, 174
Tass, Moscow, USSR, 48 *top*, 101, 163, 180
US Navy Photo donated by E. A. Phillips, Dundein, New Zealand, 90.

All other photographs by the authors.

Maps on pages *xii*, 25, and 51 by Ben Partridge

1   2   3   4   5   6   7   8   9   10

Library of Congress Cataloging in Publication Data

Cheney, Cora.
Crown of the world.

Bibliography: p.
Includes index.
SUMMARY: Surveys the history, geography, resources,
environmental problems, people, and politics of the
land inside the Arctic Circle.
1.   Arctic regions.   [1.   Arctic regions]
I.   Partridge, Ben, 1915–   joint author.   II.   Title.
G606.C48   919.8   78–22426
ISBN 0–396–07677–7

To all the people of many nations who helped us on our often arduous but never dull circumpolar expedition, this book is affectionately dedicated.

Contents

Foreword

There are several definitions of the geographic arctic, but this book will deal with the land, water, and people within the Arctic Circle and is intended for the general reader.

Cora Cheney and Ben Partridge

CROWN OF THE WORLD
A View of the Inner Arctic

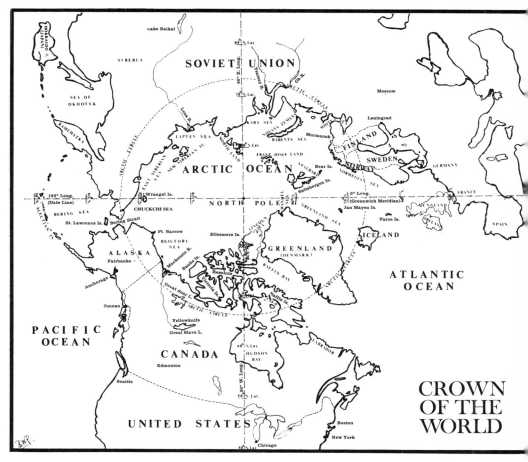

The top of the world

1

The Inuit Circumpolar Conference

++

We have an uncommon ceiling in the bedroom of our Vermont farmhouse. It is papered with a giant-sized map of the world—not just an ordinary map, but a polar projection, which means that the North Pole is in the center of the ceiling, the Arctic Circle lies around it, and the rest of the world leads to it.

We looked at the world from that unusual point of view for so many years that the polar area became an obsession. We had each seen something of the far north, mostly from airplanes, and had done a bit of camping in arctic Scandinavia. Once we had lived for a while in Iceland, long enough to make us curious about what lay north of that country. We talked about the arctic, dreamed about it, and read about it, yearning for a single book that would tell us about the people and the environment within the magic circle.

So one morning we looked at each other and said, "Let's go find out for ourselves." It was not easy. We needed money and we needed a lot of know-how to make the arrangements, for there is no such thing as an arctic packaged tour of the sort we had in mind. There is not even much public transportation between arctic countries.

But we were determined to fill in the blanks in our minds about that intriguing arctic, and a year later we set out with tents and backpacks, food and a little fear, in a sturdy Jeep and drove to Yellowknife, in Canada's Northwest Territories, literally the end of the road.

We stored the car in Yellowknife and, boarding a plane, we flew north to Tuktoyaktuk, a village where the great Mackenzie flows into the Arctic Ocean. In a biting wind we set up our tent on the frozen ground, near the tiny airport. At last we were finally standing beside the Arctic Ocean, a long way from the map on the ceiling at home.

Although it was June, the ocean was still frozen, but there were leads, or openings, in the ice. We shivered, but with our

1

warm clothes we found we could take the cold. We walked to the village and discovered what we would find over and over in the next year and half, that Eskimos are friendly people who do not live in icy igloos or constantly wear fur garments. They have grocery stores, drink soda pop, and wear blue jeans. They have many of the same problems that beset the rest of the world, plus a good many more that the rest of the world doesn't know about.

A friendly Eskimo girl who spoke English fell in step with us.

"We call ourselves Inuit," she said. "It means 'the people.' The Inuit are going to sponsor a conference where representatives of all the people within the Arctic Circle are invited to meet."

We listened eagerly as she told us that it would be held in Alaska the following June. Maybe we could be there, we thought. Nothing seemed impossible at that moment.

We spent the summer learning to live and living to learn things arctic in Canada's northern islands. In the autumn we drove the tortuous road to Alaska where we spent the winter. By spring we had arranged to attend the Inuit Circumpolar Conference which would be held in Barrow, Alaska, in June. We then planned to continue our trip around the Arctic Circle, to the Soviet Union, Lapland, Spitsbergen, Iceland, and Greenland, going completely around the crown of the world.

We arrived at the Conference a few days before most of the delegates and set up our tent near the town. By now we knew that we were going to write an arctic handbook to share the things we were learning. We wanted to put into one volume the relationships of the people, the issues, resources, politics, and the history of the arctic scene viewed from the North Pole.

Imagine that you are standing at the North Pole. Look around yourself at the rim of the Arctic Circle; it is a new view of a little-known world. The gathering at the Inuit Circumpolar Conference seems a good place to start considering today's inner arctic.

++

MAYOR EBEN Hopson of Alaska's North Slope Borough, looking as remote and distinguished as an Oriental potentate, stood in the Barrow, Alaska, airport in June, 1977, surrounded by White and

Mayor Eben Hopson at the Inuit Circumpolar Conference

Eskimo aides. The dingy little wooden building was packed with milling humanity.

There were a few old Eskimo ladies with status-symbol wolverine ruffs on their embroidered velvet parkas. There were jeans-clad Eskimo teenagers lounging on the fringe—curvaceous girls with long black hair and beguiling eyes and youths with uncombed locks and motorcycle jackets. Uninhibited children darted in and out and under, squealing, as the jet roared into the runway, transporting more people to the northernmost town in the United States.

Cameras in the hands of amateurs and professionals began snapping. Journalists and other media people, poised with notebooks and tape recorders, watched the entrance as the arriving passengers jammed into the building, pushing some of the crowd onto the muddy street outside. The gathering had begun for the first Inuit Circumpolar Conference, bringing together the Inuit, or Eskimo, people of the north. Some Natives dislike the term *Eskimo*, which means "eater of raw meat" in an Indian dialect; the Canadian Natives particularly prefer to be called Inuit, a word that simply means "the people" in their language.

3

Print from 1890's textbook shows old Lapp life-style.

More than five hundred people, Inuit and other arctic and subarctic guests, arrived by chartered or scheduled aircraft in the following twenty-four hours: Indians from Alaska and Canada; Lapps, or Samer people, from Norway, Finland, and Sweden in their bright red, gold, and blue attire; Greenlanders wearing slim *anorak* snow shirts; parka-clad Inuit from Canada, and Eskimos from other Alaskan villages. There were state and federal officials from Juneau and Washington; anthropologists and sociologists from France, England, and Japan. Concerned persons came from Denmark and the United Kingdom. Oil people from Edmonton and Anchorage kept a low profile, but the press and television people from Ottawa, Fairbanks, and who-knows-where brought an air of immediacy and glamour.

It was a fiesta, a Fourth of July picnic, and a political rally without parallel that was being watched by wary governments, for Native people of the arctic were meeting in a well-planned regional congress to discuss their own futures without regard for their nationalities. This was indeed more significant than a picturesque blanket toss.

Outside the airport taxis and local cars and trucks were kept busy carrying load after load of visitors the few muddy blocks to the modern school where cots were set up in classrooms for those who couldn't or wouldn't put up at the town's only hotel where the tariff could run a hundred a day. The cost of living in Barrow is about three times that of Washington, D.C.

Some of the Eskimo arrivals went to the homes of relatives who had greeted them joyfully at the airport. A few hardy Whites with packs and tents set up camp on the soggy tundra on the outskirts of town. And everybody got mud on his boots, for it was summer, and the ground above the permafrost—ground that never melts—had dissolved into black goo.

Inuit Circumpolar Conference, 1977

Registration at Inuit Circumpolar Conference

The registration at the school was handled by efficient young Eskimos who had learned the ways of conference planning at the boarding schools most of them had attended "down south." Maps, schedules, name tags, and locations of general meetings and workshops were distributed without a hitch. The mood was friendly.

Those who had come a few days early saw some frantic preparations as the town cleaned up its winter litter. Anyone who has lived in snow country knows that a horrendous mess emerges when the white cover melts. Trucks had struggled up and down the rutted streets to haul away to the open dump the junk that had spilled out of the ubiquitous prefabricated dwellings—broken electric stoves, old clothes, tin cans, and pile upon pile of black plastic "honey bags" of human excrement, for there are few flush toilets in the North American high arctic.

It was tactful to look the other way when the town's public

works tractors and shovels tried to cover up the rotting whales that lay on the Beaufort Sea beach or beside some houses where the choice section of whale skin and blubber called *muktuk* had been cut from a slab of whale and the rest of the meat put out for trash. If there had been dog teams instead of snow machines in the yards and fewer TV dinners in the local store there would have been no leftover meat, but "progress" had overtaken Barrow.

The matter of whaling is a touchy subject in Barrow, a town of less than three thousand, now at the crossroads where two conflicting civilizations are seen in sharp focus. Few people in the world today eat as their grandparents did, but this is a far more emotional concern than that. The Arctic coast people in the old days lived on whales which they used without waste. Now with the world's whales becoming scarce to the point of extinction, the International Whaling Commission has curtailed whaling. Northern Native people, claiming that they needed them for subsistance, have been allowed to continue hunting whales. Nobody wanted to discuss the matter, but the conference planners knew it would not look good on a television set in Montreal or New York to see that some, but not all, Native Alaskans were wasting whale meat while buying their food from well-equipped grocery stores. It would bear out the conservationists' claim that whaling is a rallying ethnic symbol rather than a survival necessity.

The rotting meat put a stench in the air and a pang in the heart of some visitors who knew that in some villages whaling is still a ceremonial rite by people who waste nothing. The new arrivals wanted to forget the problem in the warmth of the conference headquarters where local people and visitors, struggling with language barriers at times, met and laughed and drank coffee and ate doughnuts around the school cafeteria tables. Pretty young mothers with babies in their parka hoods, shy old ivory carvers, and men in business attire rubbed elbows as the crowds strolled through the nearby stunning new Borough headquarters building to look at exhibits of old and new Inuit art.

Although the conference was designed for a gathering of the Inuit people, Eben Hopson and his committee, whose energy sparked this meeting, had invited the other circumpolar people to

7

Mayor Eben Hopson and delegates at the speakers' table at the Inuit Circumpolar Conference

attend. The Soviet Union which has a small Eskimo population did not participate, even though the USSR owns about half the land within the Arctic Circle.

The idea for the conference had begun in 1973 when the Inuit Tapirisat, the politically active Eskimo brotherhood of Canada, helped organize the International Arctic Peoples Conference in Copenhagen. Although Alaska failed to send delegates, aboriginal people from Canada, Greenland, Scandinavia, and the Soviet Union met to pool their special arctic problems. There was little or no follow through on the meeting, as it was not organized as a continuing body. In 1975 Eben Hopson, who is probably one of Alaska's best-known and most respected Eskimos, decided not to let that idea die. His first move was to get grant money to finance a convention from Lilly Endowment, Inc. Keenly involved in Native rights, Hopson had long been one of the leaders in the Arctic Slope Native Association, which in 1965 filed claim against the United States government to over 88,000 square miles of traditional hunting land. He was now mayor of an arctic borough that covered 650 miles from Point Hope on the Chuckchi Sea to Demarcation Point on the Canadian border.

In November, 1976, a preconference planning session was held in Barrow with Alaskan, Canadian, and Greenlandic Native leaders. From the start plans were made for a continuing organization to serve as an arctic peoples' forum. The problems they planned to tackle in the first conference were language, communications, education, transportation, environmental protection, village health and sanitation, housing, energy resource development, and local government, all matters of high concern to arctic people. It was not on the agenda, but there was concern for two other high arctic problems: alcoholism and poor nutrition.

Health authorities are well aware of the Natives' love for the sugar-loaded snacks and ready mixes that have replaced the old diet of wild meat and seafood. In one remote Canadian Inuit village in 1976, the town council chartered a plane to bring a load of sugar, just sugar, to the Co-op store. By the time it was consumed a month later the nursing station estimated that each person in the village had eaten two pounds of sugar a day for thirty days. The poor teeth of the northern people are not due entirely to chewing skins to make soft leather.

Eskimos are deeply spiritual people, and the mood for the week was set on Sunday evening at a crowded trilingual church service where the hymns rolled out into the sunlit night. When Eben Hopson opened the conference at the appointed hour on Monday, June 13, 1977, delegates from Greenland, Canada, and Alaska surrounded him at the head table, along with church representatives for these countries. Observers sat in the bleachers that ringed the flag-bedecked gym. There were translators, the best of electronic recording and acoustical devices, and young Eskimos acting as pages and ushers. Representatives from the Naval Arctic Research Laboratory, the prestigious United States federal institution that had long seemed to dominate the Barrow region, were conspicuously absent: they had not been invited to participate. Nevertheless, the notorious anti-White sentiment that is sometimes featured in the American press was also conspiciously absent.

Low-cost meals in the school cafeteria where local and outside people broke bread were followed in the evenings by special cul-

9

Greenlanders entertain other Native people at Inuit Circumpolar Conference.

tural events. There was vigorous folk dancing by the Alaskans, singing by Canadians, a sophisticated mime theater performance by the Greenlanders, drumming and singing by the Lapps, and traditional Eskimo dancing with masks and drums.

The dissidents were there too: Charles "Etok" Edwardsen, Jr., Alaska's well-publicized young radical leader; a few Greenlanders who wanted independence from Denmark; some Canadians who dreamed of a break-off territory of their own; the Lapps who sang of their ancient lost heritage.

When the five-day conference ended, seventeen resolutions were adopted, ranging from drafting and adopting a charter to calling upon governments to recognize the aboriginal land rights of the Inuit. They asked for Inuit control of environmental policy and safe use of the arctic region, with no nuclear weapons or waste to be introduced into their territory. They wanted a voice in health and governmental matters concerning arctic villages, and they called for better transportation and communication, exchange programs, and freedom of Inuit movement over international boundaries. They called on the International Whaling Commission to defend Inuit whaling and for governments to recognize and amend treaties to aid Native hunting rights, at the same time reminding Natives to "behave as hunters" and conserve game. It was resolved that the Inuit language would be the official language in the future meetings of the Conference.

Mostly, the Inuit and other arctic people wanted their culture and their environment protected and respected. They wanted their governments, geographically so close but politically so different, to work out an arctic policy that would solve some of the special arctic problems. The Conference, they believed, had made the world more conscious of the needs of people in the far north.

2

The Arctic Circle:
North Poles and Compasses

✦✦✦

Our ceiling map at home had given us a good picture of the geography of the inner arctic. We knew that many kinds of land lay within the Arctic Circle and that seven nations controlled it. But smelling its sweet glacial air, sitting on its spongy grass, walking on its ice, and feeling its magnetic energy (or did we imagine that?) sent us searching for answers to questions we hadn't dreamed of before.

Who put that point in the center of our map and declared it to be the North Pole, and why? we pondered. Nature's magnetic pole wandered hundreds of miles away from the steady geographic North Pole that was shown on our ceiling.

At Resolute, on Canada's Cornwallis Island, we talked with American and Canadian scientists who constantly monitor the position of the magnetic north pole. They answered a lot of our questions when we popped into their warm headquarters and gratefully accepted the cup of coffee that they offered us. Tents do get cold.

✦✦✦

"YOU MAY get your certificate for crossing the Arctic Circle from the stewardess," says a voice over the loudspeaker as airborne passengers peer 25,000 feet downward at an immense cloud bank that obscures the world below.

Or, if the flying is lower and the day is clear, passengers can see bare mountains, glaciers, snow, and streams that curl in horse-

Snow-patched mountains descend to Pangnirtung Pass on Baffin Island.

shoe bends through the black, bleak, marshy land of the tundra. There is a possibility, too, of seeing trees and grass-covered farmland where cattle graze near brightly colored clusters of houses, or even sizable cities with busy ports and highrise buildings, all within the Arctic Circle.

A man-made dotted line around the top of a globe, the Arctic Circle lies at 66°33′N, like a necklace guarding the North Pole. By whose authority does this arbitrary boundary sit crownlike atop the map? What indeed does "Arctic Circle" mean?

It began with the ancient people of the northern hemisphere who looked up at the night sky and saw the steady North Star with its group of seven related heavenly bodies revolving counterclockwise around it. We call it the Big Dipper, but it seemed to imaginative ancient astronomers to have the shape of a bear; so the Greeks called the constellation the Great Bear, and we took

The early Greeks advanced the theory that the earth spun on an axis.

the modern word "arctic" from the Greek word for bear. (Tantalizing idea: Some American Indians also called the group of stars the Great Bear. Was there early communication between the North American Indians and the Greeks?)

The Greeks had even more to do with the Arctic Circle. Two centuries before the Christian era, Greek astronomers had advanced the theory that the earth revolved around the sun and spun on an axis. They even estimated the size of the earth with fair accuracy. But it took Ptolemy, a brilliant Greek scholar, to seek out the old ideas in the celebrated library at Alexandria, Egypt, and to add his genius to come up with the first orderly system of geography about eighteen centuries ago.

Ptolemy compiled the concepts of latitude and longitude, the North and South Poles, and tables for map-making and navigation, among other original mathematical theories. By today's standards his work is full of errors, but the idea of an Arctic

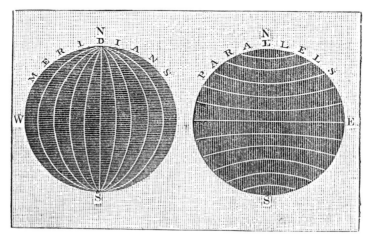

Lines of longitude and latitude

The sun's rays in the different zones, from an old textbook

Circle where lines of longitude grow closer until they converge at the North Pole, 90°N, seems first to have been recorded by Ptolemy. When the Greek and Roman civilizations fell, and barbarians who sneered at academic matters seized Europe in the Dark Ages, Ptolemy's geographic ideas were lost to the West, but the Arab world kept them alive. Later they were rediscovered by European explorers and navigators in the Middle Ages.

Now we know that since the axis of the earth tilts a bit, an area of land around the geographic North Pole is turned slightly but constantly toward the sun for six months of the year and turned away from it for the other six months. If you put the sharp end of an ordinary divider or drawing compass on the North Pole of a polar projection map and move your pencil about 23.5 degrees and draw a circle, you will have marked the Arctic Circle and enclosed the surprisingly varied geographic region that lies within it. Your pencil will show the line where there is a total of twenty-four hours of sun about June 21 and a total of twenty-four hours of no sun about December 21. At the geographic North Pole itself the sun is never above the horizon in winter or below it in summer, an idea that tickles the imagination of people who live in temperate zones.

At the vernal equinox, on June 21, the sun is at its highest point over the North Pole; at the autumnal equinox, on December 21, the sun is farthest away from it, making total darkness. Between the Pole itself and the Arctic Circle there is, of course, a proportionate gradation of seasonal light or darkness resulting in the mystic arctic twilight even when the sun is below the horizon. Joy bursts within the Arctic Circle when the sun comes over that horizon for the long day. Plant and animal life explode into frantic activity, for the earth and its creatures know that an equally long night of winter will return all too soon.

From the map maker's point of view the geographic North Pole is the true North Pole, a special spot all steady and tidy where the lines of longitude meet on the map. From this point a person could only travel south, if a person were there, which is not very often. Yet people do get there, by United States submarines, dog sleds, airplanes, and other means. The Soviet nuclear-powered icebreaker, the *Arktika*, is said to have broken the ice to the geographic North Pole in August, 1977.

Those who navigate in the north are aware of a second pole, the magnetic north pole, that has furrowed the brows of sailors and confused readers, tempting them to skip over a few paragraphs. But don't; understanding the magnetic north pole is important to the knowledge of the arctic and the problems that have beset the explorers of the north since unrecorded time.

Imagine that there is a powerful magnet in the center of the earth not quite aligned with the axis of the earth. That means its northern point of attraction on the surface would not be the same as the orderly, man-devised, geographic North Pole at 90°N. To complicate matters further, that mysterious force is constantly in motion so the magnetic north pole cannot be pinpointed on a fixed spot for any significant length of time. It can be on either land or water. In the 1970's the magnetic north pole was in the area of Cornwallis and Bathurst islands in the Canadian arctic.

A navigator in the northern hemisphere, using a magnetic compass whose needle turns north by magnetic attraction, is in a messy predicament, for maps and charts are normally based upon the geographic or true North Pole. What the map calls north disagrees with the magnetic compass, whose needle seeks out its master, the forever shifting magnetic north pole. Furthermore,

FAR LEFT: *James Clark Ross, polar explorer*

ABOVE: *Old print shows ship in the pack ice.*

there are minor differences in various parts of the earth where the compass is attracted to magnetic lines that do not invariably lead straight to the poles. (In the southern hemisphere, of course, the magnetic attraction is to the South Pole.)

The magnetic compass itself was a marvel of man's ingenuity. Instead of wandering without direction, a ship could be guided north by following the magnetized needle of the mariner's compass that pointed north. Although there is argument as to which of the early cultures—Chinese, European, Arab, or other— produced the first compass, it is known that it was used by sailors in the Middle Ages. Before the time of Columbus, seamen had deduced that there was a magnetic north pole that caused a "variation" in compass readings.

A handsome Scotsman, James Clark Ross, discovered and marked the magnetic north pole in 1831 while on an expedition commanded by his uncle. Their ship, the *Victory*, was stuck in ice, and Ross, knowing that the magnetic north pole existed, left

17

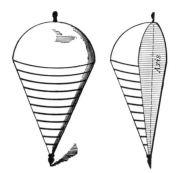

*A gyroscope works
rather like a top.*

the ship and went over the ice with Eskimo companions until his compass needle stopped moving. He knew he had located the elusive magnetic north pole.

The discovery of the magnetic north pole, then on the Boothia Peninsula in the Canadian arctic, still did not solve the problem of compass variations for navigators. Man had to put his mind to work to outwit the forces of earth's magnetism as well as the magnetic distortion caused by the steel ships that had eventually replaced wooden hulls. In the first decade of the 1900's, inventors found that the answer was to overlook magnetism as a navigational factor. Enter the gyroscope, a device with a spinning disk, rather like a child's toy top driven by an electric motor, with its axis fixed in a north-south position. It will spin to overcome the magnetic force created by the earth's rotation and still keep its direction.

Nowadays all ships of any size use gyrocompasses; yet many hold on to their magnetic compasses for emergency navigation in case of electrical failure. But, of course, early European explorers who set their prows north, following the Polar Star, never dreamed of such wonders to come.

3

Who Owns the Arctic?

++

Our ceiling map showed that most of the area within the
Arctic Circle is water and ice. Even the countries that own
land around the ocean often have ice attached to their shores
all or part of the time. Gazing out from our tent flap we wondered who had control over this land and water and the
ever-changing ice that is neither water nor land.

++

THE UNITED States, Canada, Denmark's Greenland, Iceland,
Norway, the Soviet Union, Sweden, and Finland all have land
within the Arctic Circle, but the latter two have no Arctic Ocean
seacoast. Most countries that have a coastline on the Arctic or its
ring of seas generally claim a 12-mile offshore limit, their own
continental shelf, and some form of 200-mile resource claim and
pollution-control zone. Numerous changing national policies and
treaties between nations have set specific terms for fishing and
other near shore use.

Although it is not tested by any court or agreed to by all the
nations involved, there has long been a "polar sector" or "pie"
theory of arctic jurisdiction, authority over an area. Beginning at
the North Pole, the lines of longitude that touch the east and west
tips of the nations bordering on the Arctic Ocean ascribe to each
country a triangular slice of the "pie." But the Native people who
have been in the arctic for thousands of years and have lived on

19

The Confederate raider Shenandoah

or used the ice and land and water disagree with this and feel that they have a special claim based on traditional uses. The United States holds that the Arctic Ocean is high seas, which means water that is open to vessels of all nations. This becomes a knotty problem when one considers that most of the ocean is covered with ice that can be inhabited.

A bizarre instance of using the Arctic Ocean as high seas is a little known series of sea battles that took place between the Confederate raider *Shenandoah* and some luckless Yankee whalers at the end of the American Civil War in 1865. When Alaska was Russian territory, American whaling ships freely went through the Bering Strait into the Arctic Ocean seeking the bowhead whales that were then abundant in the arctic. Confederate Lieutenant James Waddell in his smart sail- and steam-powered vessel decided to strike at the Union ships where it would hurt— their rich whaling enterprises that brought wealth into New England ports. Waddell surprised the Yankees and captured and burned one ship after another, filling his ship with prisoners and putting others ashore. There was only one flaw. The war was over, but Waddell didn't know it. In vain the captured men told him the Confederacy had surrendered, but Waddell kept on until he had seized thirty-eight whaling ships and taken over a thousand prisoners. He was on his way south to seize the city of San Francisco when a British sea captain finally persuaded him that the Rebel cause was indeed dead. The *Shenandoah* took down the Stars and Bars and returned to England, where she had been built, and her crew turned themselves in to the American consul.

Another, the Partridge theory of polar jurisdiction, is that the Arctic Ocean is divided into three layers: air, surface, and subsurface. Each has its own special jurisdiction. The sea under the ice is high seas, available to all. But the habitable polar ice has landlike qualities, even though it moves and erodes and grows. Some of the ice is attached to land, actually forming an extension of territory. So the polar ice could be regarded as something similar to land. The third layer, the air over the arctic, is space, subject to the claims of the arctic nations, and most nations of the world claim sovereignty of the air over their land to the altitude to which a manned aircraft can operate and to varying horizonal distances for defense purposes.

International lawyers agree on one point: arctic jurisdiction, which at first glance may not seem important to many people, is in any case a mess. A classic instance of muddled jurisdiction is the Fletcher's Island or T-3 murder, which took place on a "tabular berg" or floating ice island. (T-3 is a military term meaning radar target number three). Briefly, an isolated group of American civilian workers, carrying out scientific experiments for the United States government on a floating mass of ice, staged a drunken brawl. General consumption of a lethal brew of 190 proof ethyl alcohol cut with homemade raisin wine, plus human tempers, guns, and stir-crazy, loosely governed men, ended in a fatal shooting.

The ice itself was believed to have broken off Canada's Ellesmere Island ice shelf, because of certain leaves, moss, and even the caribou antlers and bodies of lemmings and other land animals that were found. It was then floating in the Canadian sector of the high seas of the Arctic Ocean. But the ice island flew, unchallenged, a United States flag. When the shooting took place,

Icebergs from the Greenland ice cap

terrified men notified American officials who sent a helicopter, since it was July and the warmer weather prevented heavier aircraft from landing. (The helicopter had to be refueled in midair, a dangerous operation.) The chopper took the alleged murderer and the dead body to Greenland. A United States military plane then flew them to an airport in Virginia, where the Federal District Court took jurisdiction over the trial.

After a complicated trial, appeal, and retrial, the defendant was acquitted in 1972. Ironically the acquittal had nothing to do with jurisdiction. However, lawyers and interested parties all over the world had watched this unprecedented case closely, hoping that some decision on ice jurisdiction would result.

Canada, which might have claimed jurisdiction, waived it. Denmark, in whose Greenland territory the helicopter with the accused had first landed, might have intervened. Fletcher's Island had a slight status as a military area, but this angle was not pursued. It was argued that an ice island was like a United States ship and hence was subject to its high seas law for vessels afloat, but a ship is navigated, and an ice island is a free-floating body. Or was T-3 a derelict vessel? But it was not abandoned. And so the arguments went, without decisions.

Suppose the people involved had been foreign nationals on this United States occupied ice? So many "what ifs" arose in the minds of the concerned officials that it was evident that arctic jurisdiction was more muddled than ever.

4

Beringea: The Lost Land Bridge and Other Archaeology

++

Sometimes at our house we think that people can be divided into two classes: those who have such a passion for archaeology that they will endure any hardship to gaze at a special hole in the ground or a particular stack of rocks; and those who think the whole thing is a bore, including the archaeologists.

But to the two of us, who belong to the passionate lunatic fringe of rock and hole lovers, finding out about arctic archaeology was the most rewarding part of our circumpolar discoveries. We were ecstatic to find ourselves camping a few feet from the ruins of ancient Eskimo dwellings in Alaska and Canada, and to discover what we believed were the foundations of Viking longhouses on Ellesmere Island.

We talked long hours with generous archaeologists in Alaska, Canada, Greenland, Lapland, and the Soviet Union. Hundreds of artifacts in arctic museums showed the relationships and movements of the early people in the north. In the Soviet city of Khabarovsk, a young woman archaeologist, speaking with excitement through an interpreter, showed us items excavated near the Amur River that were clearly related to the Eskimo culture of St. Lawrence Island in Alaska. Eyes sparkled.

Perhaps the most important thing we learned was that archaeologists, amateur or professional, speak the same language of curiosity about the past, no matter what words they use.

++

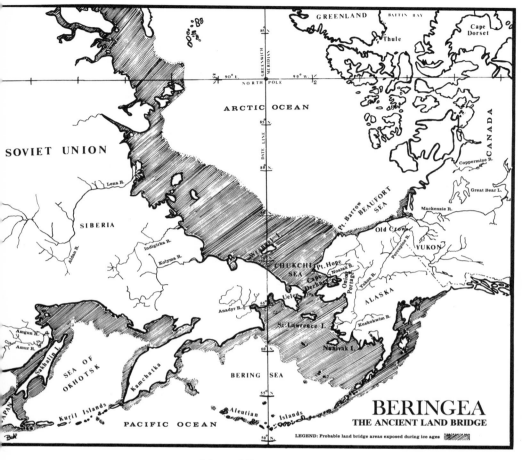

Map of Beringea

IF YOU look up the word Beringea in most dictionaries, you won't find a definition, for it is a rather new word. But the people who live in and study about the arctic know Beringea as the water, the islands, and the seacoast around the Bering Sea and the Chuckchi Sea. A continental shelf lies there between Asia and North America, roughly bordered on the south by the chain of Aleutian Islands and on the north by the Arctic Ocean. Beringea centers around the Bering Strait, the 55-mile strip of water that today separates Alaska and Siberia. Once this was a land bridge and a

25

Old map makes it easy to see location of Bering land bridge.

scene of frantic activity of migration by men and beasts in the long ago, early mists of the world.

A sea-bottom map of today shows the Beringea area to be so shallow that it is easy to imagine that the continents were once connected. They could be connected again if the water level went down less than two hundred feet.

Local people have no doubt that the land bridge once existed. The islands that lie between Siberia and Alaska were evidently peaks of land in the old bridge. On clear days people can see Siberia from America's St. Lawrence Island, one of the Bering Sea islands.

The people on St. Lawrence and their nearest Soviet neighbors share a common language, Siberian Yupik. In today's modern St. Lawrence school, where English is taught as a second language, the younger pupils use books adapted from old Soviet Eskimo-language textbooks. Before modern international complications made socializing impossible, the Eskimos of the Alaskan and Siberian coasts met and traded freely.

Studies of the geology and climate of the dim past tell a story of how the migrations of animals and people were made possible. The stage is set in the Pleistocene or Glacial epoch of the world's development, which began about half a million to two million years ago. Human beings were on earth during the Pleistocene epoch, and Paleolithic or Stone Age people lived in Asia then.

Anthropologists, who study the origins and behavior of mankind, and archaeologists, who study the physical evidences of human life from the past, have many theories about the Stone Age migrants from Asia. They were not all the same kind of people, for some belonged to different groups of the human species.

It is generally believed that northeast Asia was first inhabited by the Caucasoid people, which includes most American Indians. These Asian Caucasoids were gradually driven north by tough and warlike Mongoloid people from China.

In the Pleistocene epoch of the world, when great geological changes were taking place, so much of the earth's water was tied

Waterfront scene, Kotzebue, Alaska, on Chuckchi Sea, one of the earliest spots where man arrived in North America from Asia

A glacier meets the ocean at Spitsbergen causing mists and clouds over the mountain peaks.

up in mighty ice caps and glaciers that the sea level dropped. The shallow water between Asia and North America turned into a land bridge that was at times two hundred or more miles wide.

As the water gradually dropped, animals began moving into the newly emerging bridge to escape persistent hunters with their stone weapons. To find better hunting than Asia offered, and to avoid the pressure of the Mongoloid tribes, the Caucasoid people followed the animals to this new territory.

These earliest people were probably the ancestors of the American Indians. They began moving across Beringea at least thirty thousand years ago, and probably earlier. Many ages later the Mongoloid people came across the Beringea bridge. These later people were the ancestors of today's Eskimos or Inuit.

Before and with the people came camels, bisons, wild horses, as well as saber-toothed tigers, mastodons, mammoths, and other prehistoric animals that are extinct now, and other animals whose descendants still live on the two American continents.

The migrations across Beringea went on over hundreds of centuries. There was not just one period of glaciation or ice age in the Pleistocene epoch; there were at least four periods when the world was so cold that the water was frozen into great glaciers and the sea level dropped for thousands of years to make the bridge appear. And then for some reason, not quite solved by scientists, the world would warm up again, and water from melted ice would cover the land bridge.

The last bridge that would support a mass migration was flooded about ten thousand years ago, cutting off the movement of people from Asia to North America.

Layers of fossils of marine creatures that came from the Pacific Ocean into the Arctic Ocean and to the North Atlantic help geologists date the rise and fall of the bridge as it came and went through the ages, bringing its various waves of people and animals. So far no human remains have been found under the water of Beringea, but bones and artifacts on eroded beaches give a

Weathered whalebone ruins of ancient dwelling at Point Hope, Alaska, emerge from the sod and snow.

The early peoples in the arctic built their homes of stones, bones, and ice because they had no wood. Pictured here in today's Alaska is a

record of the migrations. There have been some unsuccessful attempts at underwater research, and someday soon a scholar in a wetsuit may find out more precise knowledge of prehistoric people in Beringea.

When the various groups of people moved into North America onto the cold arctic beaches, they kept moving south if the climate permitted, as during some of the earth's history ice blocked the passages south. Some of the earliest people who stayed in the arctic were the Athapascan Indians of the Alaskan and Canadian interior. Other Indians were able to get to more moderate climates. Finally there were people in the southern tip of South America whose ancestors had come across the land bridge. It is estimated that it would have taken seven thousand years for generations of people moving three miles a year to cover that distance.

The Eskimos who came on the last land bridge were blocked into the north by enemies to the south and by ice barriers. So they

more recently abandoned dwelling constructed of sod, whalebone, and driftwood.

spread east around the Arctic Ocean all the way to Greenland and along Alaska's northwest coast. They were already adapted to cold weather with their tough stocky bodies, eyes protected by extra fat, and coarse, thick hair. They became even hardier, for only the fittest survived. Some of the Eskimos lived on the ice itself, feeding themselves on sea mammals and using bones and ice for building material, for they had no wood.

Modern researchers have reconstructed this story by studying language patterns, among other things. The Indians in the interior of Canada and Alaska speak a language that is similar to that spoken by Indians in the lower United States and even in South America. Eskimos and Indians speak a different language.

Excavations that turn up bones and tools are other clues to the movements of people. When the Alcan Highway was built during World War II, a trail of remains of ancient travelers showed the path taken by some of the Indians. At Old Crow, in Canada's Yukon Territory, a human bone was found in an archaeological excavation in 1976 which was estimated to be twenty thousand years old. Old Crow, on the Porcupine River, is probably the oldest permanent settlement in the Americas.

The detective work of arctic archaeologists is a story of dedication and daring. There have been as many theories and as many names given to sites and cultures as there have been researchers, it would seem. But in general the story of the land bridge and the movement of people in Beringea over the ages from Asia to North America is agreed upon.

Although weather and frozen ground make excavations difficult, the arctic is an archaeologist's delight since matter deteriorates so slowly in the cold climate. On Devon Island in the Canadian arctic, for example, tins of beef, tools, and clothing left by explorers a century ago are as good as new. Pieces of wood a thousand years old have been found well preserved, and the meat of extinct animals has been uncovered in the ice.

In 1939, three noted archaeologists, Froelich Rainey, Helge Larsen, and Louis Giddings, examined ruins at Point Hope, Alaska, in the Beringea area. In the early 1920's, Knud Rasmussen, a Greenlander with Inuit ancestry, made a three-year expedition by dog team from Greenland to Siberia. He had paused at Point Hope and noted the many remains of early people, wondering if this might be the original home of all Inuit people, a theory since discarded. However, Rasmussen's report of the many antiquities he found interested the three scientists. They were distressed that a well-meaning Christian missionary had buried over four thousand prehistoric skulls in a fever of religious zeal, but they found Point Hope a fascinating place to uncover some mysteries of the past.

With the world facing total war there was little general interest in archaeology, but in 1940 Dr. Rainey, who was then at the University of Alaska, and a few helpers returned to Point Hope to do a little more work on this site. In a dramatic moment of arctic history, Dr. Rainey, looking out at the summer snow-free earth, recognized patterns in the grass and mosses that made him suddenly sense that here was an ancient city, laid out with streets, with perhaps eight hundred house sites on the land that sloped to

Indian woman at Old Crow in Canada's Yukon. This settlement on the Porcupine River is one of the oldest continuously occupied spots in North or South America.

Indian child plays on the banks of the Porcupine River in Canada's Yukon. Her ancestors may have lived here for more than 20,000 years.

Inuit graves, Ellesmere Island

the sea. Excavations revealed a culture that he had first believed to be over a thousand years old. The artifacts in the graves were not even familiar to the Native people who helped with the work. There were buried bodies with artificial eyes of ivory plugged into the empty eye sockets. Some experts thought this was from ancient Chinese influence. At Point Hope, as at other Alaskan seaside sites, there are doubtless scientifically rich ruins under water because the ocean has eroded the former shore during the centuries.

The discovery of radiocarbon dating in the 1940's revolutionized archaeology. Radiocarbon or carbon 14 dating, developed at the University of Chicago, is based on the fact that all living matter accumulates radioactivity in its life-span but loses it at a predictable rate after death. Living matter, such as wood, charcoal, bones, and plant life, can be prepared in certain labora-

Ruins of ancient Inuit dwellings, Ellesmere Island

Detail of ancient Inuit dwelling, Ellesmere Island

tory processes so that the present rate of radiation can be measured and the age of the object computed. Since rocks are not composed of living cells, a stone tool can only be dated if it is found attached to or beside a piece of charcoal or bone that can be estimated to be of the same age. Arrowheads or stone objects which are taken from sites cannot be authentically dated, which is why trained archaeologists plead with the public not to move anything from an excavation or suspected ancient location.

When the Point Hope or Ipiutak finds were subjected to the radiocarbon-dating tests, they were found to be much older than at first estimated. The ancient city is probably over three thousand years old and may have had a population of four thousand or more.

In the 1950's work in arctic archaeology went forward rapidly. Probably the most important feat in that decade was the late Dr. Louis Giddings' discovery of a stratified site at Onion Portage on Alaska's Kobuk River. Actually the intrepid Dr. Giddings, who insisted on tramping the arctic region alone or sailing swift rivers on rafts, marked the site in 1941 when he was seeking ancient wood on which he could use his specialty of dating by tree rings. He was rafting down the Kobuk when he stopped at the ancient portage and found some promising prospects. Twenty years later he returned and found, on this inland site, the stratified remains of multiple cultures. By 1964, with the support of Brown University, Giddings had found evidence of eight layers of civilization at this crossing, dating back to perhaps thirteen thousand years ago. Some of the layers seem to hold Athapascan Indian remains as well as Eskimo. There are many more Eskimos than Indians in the arctic, and they have traditionally been hostile to each other, although there are now Eskimo/Indian communities, especially around Canada's Mackenzie River.

Amateurs turn up ancient items, too, but there are now laws forbidding removing them in all arctic countries. Sometimes the Inuit people have been the worst offenders, for old mastodon or whale ivory bone brings high prices when it is carved and sold. In 1975 the Canadian government made a sensible deal to the advantage of everyone when the National Museum of Man and the

Department of Indian and Northern Affairs decided that they should help make the bone and ivory available to carvers and at the same time get the archaeological information they needed. The institutions sent parties into several areas of the Canadian north to mark "Thule" culture sites, an ancient Inuit culture noted for its use of whalebone in building houses, boats, and sleds. Experts examined the sites, took the information, and then made the bone available to modern carvers, a unique experiment in the arctic.

Since 1971 the Alaska Native corporations have controlled their ancestral land, and nobody may excavate or disturb antiquities without permission of the village authorities. In 1972, near Savoonga on St. Lawrence Island, only 40 miles from the Soviet Union and 118 miles from Alaska, two Eskimo hunters found the oldest intact body ever located in the Americas. The frozen, mummified cadaver had slipped from its grave in an eroded cliff. Later, with the permission of the village council, the United States National Park Service, which was consulted, turned the

Ruins of ancient sod, whalebone, and stone dwelling are protected by law on Ellesmere Island as elsewhere in the arctic, but amateur archaeologists may observe them.

Godthab, Greenland's capital city, lies just below the Arctic Circle. Present-day concentration of people into large cinderblock apartment buildings has brought a host of problems.

body over to the University of Alaska. After an autopsy and extensive examination by a number of institutions, it was determined that the body was that of a woman who had met a violent death, probably trapped in her house in a landslide or earthquake sixteen hundred years ago. The body was reverently treated and returned to the Eskimos on St. Lawrence Island for burial in the summer of 1977.

Greenlandic and Danish archaeologists have for years studied and excavated old Eskimo sites, especially those of the ancient Sarqaq and later Thule cultures which flourished in Greenland. At Greenland's capital city, Godthaab (pronounced God-hope), a new museum specializing in Greenlantic antiquities was opened in 1977.

The Soviets have done massive archaeological research among the arctic Native people since the days of the Russian czars. Foreigners are not often admitted into the Soviet north, but there are available studies. The key to Eskimo origins seems to lie within the Soviet Union. At the Museum of Local History in Khabarovsk in the Soviet Far East there are displays from excavations around the Amur, Angara, and Aldan Rivers and from Kamchatka. Museum experts believe that one of these areas may have been the original home of the Eskimos. Recent work on the Aldan River has turned up evidence of humans in Siberia 33,000 to 35,000 years ago, predating mankind in the Americas. At Uelen, across the Bering Straight from Alaska, grave excavations have also revealed an Eskimo culture far older than any remains found in North America.

The Soviets now have a number of regional museums of Native culture of the far north, but many artifacts have been taken to larger museums in Leningrad and Moscow. The Institute of Arctic Studies in Leningrad has material about the early arctic groups which include Eskimos, Evenks, Chuckchi, Yakuts, Nenets, Ngansans, Dolgans, Yukagirs, Lapps, and other lesser known tribes.

In spite of centuries of study, archaeologists and anthropologists still do not know positively about the origin of the Samer or Lapp people who live above the Arctic Circle on the Kola Peninsula in the Soviet Union and across upper Scandinavia. Although the dating is debatable, excavations of stone-age sites indicate that people may have lived there 8000 years ago. There are even remains of wooden skis 2500 years old, of the type used by Lapps today. In any case, early historians noted contact with aboriginal northern tribes 1900 years ago. It is generally believed that these people originated in central Europe and went north in search of game or were driven there by more aggressive groups. They may have become isolated by climatic conditions and developed their own unique cultures centering around reindeer herding, hunting, and fishing. Cut off from the rest of Europe, they lived their nomadic lives until the strong Norse and Russian civilizations from the south encroached on them. Today Lapps seem more culturally than physically related for they have highly differing features and blood types. Of course, there has been a great deal of intermarriage and assimilation into the neighboring populations. Their ancient language, which has nine distinct dialects, is Finno-

Old print shows traditional Lapp home

Ugraic, unrelated to the Eskimo and Indian tongues.

Although Lapps have no known relationship to the Eskimos or Indians, all three shared some customs, such as the use of drums and ceremonial masks, bear-killing rites, and their belief in shamans or witch doctors who could perform miraculous feats. Since many Lapps lived where there were trees they made bread of tree bark. Archaeologists have found that they worshiped holy stones and carved tree stumps. They lived in fur tents or yurts made of earth and bark and dressed in furs as did the ancient people of North America.

There were no Native people in Iceland or Spitsbergen when Europeans began to invade the north in historic times. Archaeologically, the arctic seems not to be a cradle of mankind, but human beings did move into the land within the Arctic Circle in the Stone Age and the descendants of some still live in the far north today.

5

The Arctic Ocean and Its Ice

++

As we traveled on, beside, and over the arctic ice, we realized that ice is many things, mysterious and constantly changing. We watched leads of open water come and go. We realized the dangers of ice when we walked on it at Ellesmere Island and within a few minutes found ourselves suddenly surrounded by open water, forcing us to take a long leap to safety. We saw awesome pressure ridges caused by surging ice along the Alaskan Chuckchi seacoast. Ice has many faces and forms that we had never imagined from simply looking at our map.

++

WHEN PEOPLE think of the crown of the world they are likely to come up with an image of solid ice. Although the amount of ice up there varies somewhat with the seasons, a mean proportion of land, water, and permanent ice within the Arctic Circle is about one-third of each—hardly an ocean of ice. Yet 15 percent of the earth's ice is within the Arctic Circle, affecting the entire world in that ice reflects rather than absorbs the sun's rays.

What is ice, other than a crystal cube from the refrigerator for a cooling drink, or a smooth surface for skating, or a curse for skidding a car into the ditch? Entire dictionaries defining ice terms have been written in a number of languages. The Eskimos, who should know, have over a hundred words for varieties of ice and snow.

41

A Baffin Island fiord at low tide catches the summer sun.

Break-up in polar ice pack

Ice is the solid state of water, and an ice crystal is formed when fresh water freezes at or below 32° F (0° C). Salt water, depending upon the degree of salinity, freezes at proportionately lower temperatures. Since each molecule of freezing water consists of two atoms of hydrogen and one atom of oxygen, the attraction of the hydrogen to the oxygen in the adjoining water molecules provides the bond that holds ice together.

There are three general classes of ice: floating ice, land ice, and atmospheric ice. All are in evidence around the Arctic Ocean most of the time.

The arctic ice pack is an example of floating ice. So are icebergs, ice floes, and ice islands. If floating ice is attached to shore it is known as fast ice, and it provides a surface, sometimes smooth and sometimes ridged by pressure, for hunting or exotic hiking.

Pressure ridges in polar ice pack—floating ice

Hanging glacier and constant mist in rocky cliffs on Baffin Island

Snow does not always destroy a day of fun in the arctic.

Land ice includes glaciers, ice caps, and even the never-melting permafrost.

Atmospheric ice, most familiar to people who live in more temperate climates, ranges from freezing drizzle, to snow, to sleet, to hail, to ice fog or air filled with frozen crystals.

A glance at any Arctic Ocean map shows that most of it is labeled permanent ice pack. This permanent ice is not stationary

Iceberg, spring leads, and floes

Iceberg in sea ice

or even continuous, for it shifts, moves, and is often separated by open water.

Icebergs, the floating sculpture of the frost giants, join the other sea ice to become part of the polar ice pack unless they are borne by currents out of the Arctic Ocean to bedevil ships in North Atlantic waters. Sometimes when walking on ice, leaping over cracks and fissures, one can see small icebergs at close hand. Down through the clear Arctic water the submerged portion of the iceberg seems even more intricately detailed than the surface portion.

For some people the most bizarre of the units in the ice pack are the ice islands, which are also known as tabular bergs, massive flat-topped icebergs that have broken off from an ice shelf or a thick area of shore-attached ice. In August, 1946, when the arctic air was crisscrossed with aircraft, a United States Air Force plane, flying over the Arctic Ocean, saw a new and uncharted island in the sea below. Later investigations showed that it was an ice island, fifteen by eighteen miles in area, moving north through the ice pack. Planes began to watch and plot this unusual floating formation and to look out for other such features. At least a hundred more ice islands have been discovered since, ranging from less than a mile in length to others the size of the first discovery. At last here was an explanation of the many mysterious islands that explorers had found in the past and that were never again located—they were moving islands of ice.

Americans were not the only modern travelers to discover ice islands. In 1946, the Soviet icebreaker *Mikoyan* not only found but sent a party ashore on an ice island. With aviation opening the way to arctic research to a degree that had never been possible before, imaginative people began to think of setting up observation bases on these floating islands. Soviet explorers had already landed planes on ice floes, and the Americans were eager to go even further.

Iceberg, floe, and shorefast ice

A Russian plane lands on an ice island in 1976.

In March, 1952, the world's first plane-landing on an ice island took place a hundred miles from the Pole on the previously mentioned radar target T-3, known as Fletcher's Ice Island in honor of the commander of that expedition, Lieutenant Colonel J. O. Fletcher.

Iceberg. Big tabular bergs are called ice islands.

Rotten ice

A runway was built on T-3 that allowed planes to come and go, despite the constant hazard of fog, to bring supplies and to give scientists a base for arctic studies. In the early 1960's Fletcher's Island grounded off Point Barrow, Alaska, and was later abandoned, reoccupied, and then reabandoned. It was still circling in 1978, and so are stories and plans concerning it.

Ice islands come and go, with new ones calving occasionally and old ones disappearing by breaking up or slipping from the Arctic into the warmer North Atlantic where they rot away by melting. Observation stations on them have enabled the scientific community to learn more about the climate and history of the earth and oceans in the last thirty years than was known in the last three thousand years. Some of the ocean bottom has been photographed, plant and animal life identified, and depths and features of the ocean bottom compiled. More information on ocean currents and predictions for future world climatic conditions are coming out of the arctic today at a dizzying rate.

The Arctic Ocean has been compared with the Mediterranean, for both are almost landlocked bodies of water. The two major outlets for the northern ocean are the Bering Strait to the Pacific and the Norwegian Sea to the Atlantic. A ring of seas surrounds the ocean, merging to form part of it. Clockwise, beginning with the Chuckchi Sea just north of the Bering Strait, the arctic seas are the East Siberian, Laptev, Kara, Barents, White, Norwegian, Greenland, Wandel, Lincoln, and Beaufort.

The Arctic Ocean has an average depth of 4,200 feet, but the sea-bottom valleys and mountains make that a meaningless figure. The greatest known depth is 17,000 feet. It is easier to imagine the ocean's size by realizing that the surface is five times as large as the Mediterranean.

After World War II and the rising tension between the USSR and the United States of America, both governments recognized the importance of the arctic. About 1950, Soviet scientists located the Lomonosov Ridge, a subterranean mountain that stretches from the New Siberian Islands to Greenland and Ellesmere. In an ocean depth of nine thousand to twelve thousand feet, its peaks rise to within three thousand feet of the surface. In effect, this ridge divides the Arctic basin in half, with the Eurasian Basin, surrounded loosely by the northern reaches of the Soviet Union and Greenland on one side, and the Amerasian Basin, bounded by Alaska, Siberia, and Canada on the other. Within these two basins are two distinct patterns of the movement of water, with a counterclockwise current in the Eurasian Basin and a clockwise movement in the Amerasian Basin, reminding one of opposite hair whorls on identical twins.

The Eurasian Basin, connected with the Atlantic Ocean through the Greenland and Norwegian Seas, makes an exchange of warm and cold water possible, flowing in and out between Greenland and Spitsbergen. When the cooled water returns to the Atlantic it is known as the East Greenland Current.

When Pacific waters enter and mingle with the Arctic Ocean through the Bering Strait, the exact patterns are complex and generally uncharted, but they contribute to the constant and sometimes furious currents and movements of the ocean.

Although almost half of Norway lies within the Arctic Circle, it is not as cold as the other high arctic land because the North

50

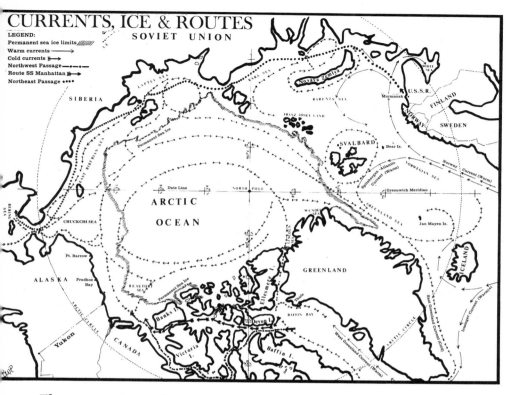

The currents, ice, and routes of the arctic

Atlantic current, an extension of the Gulf Stream, touches the Norwegian coast. East Greenland, on the other hand, is too cold for comfort because of the ice that is carried away from the Arctic Ocean along Greenland's steep shore.

The surface currents of the Arctic are only a small part of the complex movements as there are layers of varying temperatures, each with its own current peculiarities. People who live in the arctic and have trouble finding fresh water cut blocks of old sea ice which has low salt content to melt for drinking. Since fresh water freezes faster than salt water and floats above it, the land's glacial runoff and water from rivers, such as the Ob, Lena, and Yenesei from the Soviet Union and the Mackenzie from Canada, supply much of the ice cover of the Arctic Ocean.

The ocean acts as a heat reservoir.

The ocean acts as a heat reservoir for the crown of the world since the water is warmer than the land. Heat moves downward through the layered ocean with great difficulty, but when there is a lead or break in the surface ice, there is a loss of ocean heat. This means that the ocean has a moderating effect on the climate because there is a lower limit on sea water temperature: it never falls below 28° F (−2° C). The winter water remains warmer than the air in spite of the ice topping which serves to slow down the exchange of heat. If much surface ice should melt, the loss of heat from the ocean would have a great effect on the glaciers, the surrounding land, and the level of water throughout the world.

The mean annual temperature at the North Pole is estimated to be about −9° F (−23° C), but wind-chill factors make it much colder. The heat balance of the arctic water and air affects us all, for oddly enough, when there is more ice cover on the Arctic Ocean we have more cold in the rest of the northern hemisphere.

Less surface ice means more atmospheric circulation to build up nearby glaciers, leaving less moisture for us in the south. We then get a drier climate and cooler summers but on the whole a higher annual temperature.

If the average person has a hard time encompassing these complex ideas, scientists have even more trouble trying to solve this jigsaw puzzle where many of the key pieces are missing. No wonder they disagree, discuss, and change theories rather frequently; but you can count on it that the Arctic Ocean has something to do with what jacket, if any, to put on when you leave the house today.

North Pole—the top of the world

6

The Land Around the Arctic Ocean

++

We became well acquainted with arctic land because we slept on it, hiked on it, and developed a love-hate feeling when the discomfort of wet boots and the beauty of arctic flowers provided two emotions.

The pure glacial air and the occasional swarms of mosquitoes made further contrasts. Like ice, arctic land was a varied world that seemed to melt into the ocean.

++

THE LAND around the Arctic Ocean is sometimes hard to distinguish from ice, but modern mapping has defined the shores. Mainly the land is classed as taiga and tundra. Taiga is a geographic term for land where trees grow. In the arctic that includes mostly the areas around the large rivers in Canada, Alaska, and the Soviet Union, and the sea-warmed shores of Scandinavia.

The rest of the land is tundra, which has no trees because the permafront earth below it never melts. It is classed as an arctic desert since there is almost no rainfall and little snow. In summer the tundra is covered in part with mosses, lichens, grasses, and in some places with masses of wild berries that the Natives gather and store. Sorrel, a tasty green vegetable, grows wild in most

Willow tree not much larger than a hand may be a hundred years old.

arctic areas. There are even deceptive little trees, mostly willows that lie on the ground, posing as creeping plants to protect themselves from the wind. Some of them are three or four feet long, or high, depending on how you consider them, and may be one hundred years old when tested for microscopic tree rings. Arctic growth is, of course, overall very slow, taking many seasons for a flowering plant to reach the maturity to blossom. Often they are stunted miniature relatives of the flowers of the subarctic and temperate zones. Tiny wild gardens cling to appropriate rocks or soil in the brief season of light, and because the sun shines day and night the growth seems almost magic while it lasts.

There are cultivated gardens above the Arctic Circle, too. Peo-

Old print shows Hammerfest.

ple treasure window gardens and greenhouses. Of course, in Scandinavia there is commercial farming, and flower beds adorn the yards in cities such as Hammerfest and Tromsö. But the real surprises are such sights as tough little cabbages and kale and turnips that are lovingly tended by coal miners in Spitsbergen or other unlikely spots.

Greenhouses at Spitsbergen

Arctic hikers take advantage of ice for smoother footing.

Strangely, there would be no growth if it were not for the hard permafrost that distinguishes the taiga from the tundra. Permafrost acts as a container to hold the surface soil which can be from a few inches to many feet deep. This top layer of soil which holds the plants of course freezes in winter, and when the summer sun warms the surface, it melts only to the permanent layer of ice, the permafrost line. This keeps the plants watered, outwitting the

Arctic summer on Baffin Island. Glacial melt cuts rivers into gravel deposit in valley.

desert conditions that would prevail if the melted surface water could sink without restriction down into the earth. It also turns the tundra into an unholy sea of mud and a natural heaven for mosquito breeding.

When the tundra refreezes in winter, the water remaining between the top ice and the permafrost is under terrible pressure. Sometimes it erupts in "pingoes," blisters of earth that look like small volcanoes. The violence of pressured ice can even destroy a house if it is built on a weak spot of earth in deep permafrost areas.

The Soviet Union has more land bordering the Arctic Ocean than any other nation, with a vast mysterious low-lying tundra coastline stretching from Murmansk in Europe, through Asia, and ending at craggy Cape Dezhnev, which almost touches the North American continent. In addition, the USSR has a number of rocky islands in the ocean—Franz Joseph Land, Novaya Zemlya, New Siberian Islands, Wrangell Island, North Land, and other smaller ones.

Denmark's Greenland comes second in size with an inner circle area of over half a million square miles, most of which are covered by an ice cap like the one that once clutched the top of North America. The Greenland ice cap is 11,100 feet at its deepest point with an average thickness of 4,800 feet. The depth of glaciers can be measured by radio echo soundings. Greenland's Pearyland is the most northerly land on earth.

Canada's holdings above the Arctic Circle include the upper tip of the Yukon Territory and about half of the Northwest Territories, including the lacework of islands that extends from Baffin and Ellesmere on the east to the mouth of the surging Mackenzie River on the west, where the taiga meets the tundra. Ice, land, and water mingle in the Canadian islands in spectacular cold confusion.

Alaska comes next in size of the land mass that edges the cold ocean, with about one thousand miles of arctic coast. Behind the low-lying coastal tundra the Brooks Range rises. A wide-angle look from the North Pole to Alaska's coast would show oil rigs at Prudhoe where the controversial Aleyska pipeline begins. One

Rocky shore of Arctic Ocean

could also see Native fishing camps where families go to spend summer in canvas tents in their traditional fishing areas.

Finland, Sweden, and Norway lie partially within the Circle, but only Norway has an Arctic Ocean seacoast. Indented with hundreds of miles of deep fiords, it comprises about half of Norway's total coastline. Norway has further power in the Arctic with her limited sovereignty over Spitsbergen, which also has a small Soviet settlement that coexists uneasily with the Norwegian coal miners who make up the principal population.

Iceland, which lies just below the Arctic Circle, has only a small bit of arctic land, a tiny outpost, Grimsey Island, where planes from the main island land on a strip that runs directly on the Circle. Grimsey, which measures five miles long by two miles wide, is a green, hay-covered, treeless hill where shaggy sheep roam in summer. Blond, sturdy children leap over the jagged

*A classic hanging glacier,
Baffin Island*

rocks high above the strong surf, rocks where puffins and eiders and ducks can be seen. (When triplets were born in Iceland's Grimsey in 1977 its population increased from ninety-six to ninety-nine!)

Most of the land within the Arctic Circle has glaciers. These landborn glaciers seem to be one of the most alluring features of nature to arctic visitors. Broad, curving, graceful, and mysterious, a typical mountain glacier spreads in a frozen downward sweep to the sea. Technically a glacier is a mass of snow and ice continually moving from higher to lower ground, or, if it is afloat, as some glaciers are, it is continually spreading in a fan shape.

Glaciers which are not being replenished with sufficient snow at the top will retreat until further growth is possible.

Besides the familiar mountain glaciers, glaciers include valley glaciers, which flow down valleys; ice shelves, floating ice attached to a coast; ice sheets, which are thick masses of ice and snow resting on rock; ice caps, smaller, dome-shaped ice forms that generally cover a mountain area; and ice piedmonts, the ice covering of a seaward sloping strip of low land backed by mountains.

Sometimes a glacier hangs on a steep wall over a formerly glaciated valley. These spectacular ice bodies are called hanging glaciers, and in the Pangnirtung Pass on Canada's Baffin Island, intrepid backpackers can hike through the old glacial valley and see hanging glaciers on either side.

Lonely hiker and hanging glacier on Baffin Island

Hiking or climbing on glaciers is a heady, dangerous sport requiring special safety equipment. Crevasses, or cracks in the surface of glaciers, are especially hazardous. John Muir was one of the earliest glacier enthusiasts nearly a century ago when he explored glaciers in Yosemite and Alaska.

A glacier is born when there is a repeated yearly buildup of snow that exceeds the annual amount of melting, no matter what the quantity of snow. Even a little bit of snow can make a glacier if it constantly exceeds the melting. Each year the layer of surviving snow, called the "firn," has become covered with dirt, ash, pollen, or other particles from the air. When the snow of the following year falls and presses down the old snow, the debris leaves a dark line or firn line that separates the compacted layers, making it easy to tell the age of a glacier. Glaciers can also be carbon dated by radioactive testing of the deposits on the firns.

Pressure squeezes most of the oxygen out of the lower snow layers, turning them a heavenly shade of blue. This lack of oxygen causes the *ping* when glacial ice is dropped into a glass of ordinary water. It is fashionable in some restaurants to serve glacial ice at the bar, and there are even bags of glacial ice to be had at some specialty shops. Actually this is not such a new idea. For over a decade just before the Civil War, Alaskan ice was shipped to San Francisco to make ice cream for gold-rich miners. There is serious work being done now to move icebergs into arid climates for use as fresh water.

As living glaciers move along in their usually slow and steady fashion, receding or moving forward (for glaciers are considered dead if there is no movement), the surface melt creeps down into the mass and refreezes as solid ice. The old snow below becomes as solid as rock; in fact, it is rock, for a glacier is essentially an aggregate of mineral grains of the hydrogen and oxygen which composed the water from which the snow was made.

The reasons for the movement of glaciers are complex, but it is known that when most of the ice crystals are in a position so that their layers of atoms are parallel to the surface, the ice flows more easily. Sometimes glaciologists speak of a "plastic" condition at the bottom of the glacier that causes it to glide. Glaciers may

Present-day explorers cross a rampaging river of glacial run-off in Canada's Auyuittuq National Park.

move very rapidly. The Black Rapids Glacier in the Alaska Range began to advance at a rate of 220 feet a day. While the terrified owners of a roadhouse in the glacier's path watched in desperation, it continued its surging march, only to stop and recede less than a mile from the apparently doomed building. The old house on the Richardson Highway was acquired by the Alaska State Parks System in 1978 as a memorial to the miracle. At Juneau, Alaska, the famed blue Mendenhall Glacier will submerge the naturalists' headquarters building by 1991 if it continues its present trend.

Glaciers hold secrets from the past; they have given up frozen bodies of extinct animals, ancient human corpses and artifacts, and pollens and plants to help the study of the earth's history.

When a glacier reaches the ocean the higher temperature of the water causes the tip or tongue to break off, or calve. This calf, seven-eighths of which lies below the water, is an iceberg. At Jakobshavn, in Greenland, an energetic glacier sends an iceberg

Greenland ice cap churns out icebergs that eventually move into the North Atlantic.

into the ocean every five minutes, making five cubic miles of ice annually.

One of the most outlandish feats on a glacier was building the nuclear city Camp Century under the Greenland ice cap. America's large-scale ice-tunneling exploits began in 1955 when military engineers excavated a section of the edge of the ice cap near the United States Air Force Base at Thule, Greenland, using coal-mining techniques. Scientists were curious about the structure and history of the Greenland ice cap, the largest remnant of the last ice age. They reasoned that if a core sample from a sufficient depth could be analyzed it would be possible to learn more about the history of the earth firsthand than had ever been available before.

A nuclear reactor with forty-two pounds of uranium furnished the power for this experiment. There were twenty-one tunnels with a main street twelve hundred feet long. For over two years between 1960 and 1963 a population of one hundred men lived under the ice cap in a city that had steam baths, a theater, a chapel, and comfortably heated living quarters, while the temperature outside was well below 0° F (—17.8° C). They drilled nine thousand feet through the ice, reaching snow two thousand years old, and proved that Greenland was once tropical.

What caused the changes in the climate of the earth? There are many theories. Some think the earth shifted on its axis, causing the poles to move. Others believe that the earth's crust slipped around the core, changing the position of all the continents in relation to the sun. Still others think that sunspots or volcanic ash interrupted solar action causing cooling and heating. Nobody knows, but it is awesome to contemplate.

Sometimes the earth is drenched with electrified particles from the sun. When they approach the earth our magnetic force attracts them and diverts them to the magnetic poles. When they enter the earth's atmosphere they give off wavering sheets of colored prismatic lights that sweep across the sky. This is the aurora borealis, or the northern lights, that makes a person's spine tingle with wonder at the arctic heavens. Although it is argued that there is no sound attached to the spectacle, many people have heard them crackling across the magnetic north pole. It is even possible to see the aurora in daylight in a darkened sky.

There are other lesser known atmospheric phenomena at the crown of the world such as the mirages caused by the bending of the slanting sun rays. There are sun dogs and moon dogs, bright spots of light at the opposite ends of a halo around the sun or moon. Since the halo is caused by the bending rays that are passing through ice crystals in the air, these are actually tiny mirrors of crystals within the halo. Layers of cold and hot air cause objects to seem very close and then quickly disappear altogether.

At Grise Fiord on Ellesmere Island a person can look sixty miles across the water at Devon Island and within seconds watch it apparently sink into the sea. It is an optical illusion, of course, but it makes one believe, with an appropriate shiver, that ghostly things happen in the arctic ambience.

7
Exploration:
The Arctic Mystique

++

When we arrived in Tromsö, Norway, after our Arctic Ocean voyage, our minds were full of thoughts of explorers of the past. Luxuriating in a comfortable hotel, we saw from our window an impressive statue of that great Norwegian explorer, Roald Amundsen. Pigeons roosted on his shoulders and children played around his feet.

We thought of the museum dedicated to Soviet arctic exploration in Leningrad, and of the American explorers Peary and Stefansson. We thought about current explorers who are looking at the inner arctic these days by dogsled, snow machine, and on foot. Explorers from all parts of the world have followed the North Star to their destiny, and sometimes to their death.

Amundsen's burial place is not known, for he disappeared while searching for an explorer who was missing. Another awesome dimension was added to our ceiling map with its secrets of explorers over the ages.

++

ARCTIC EXPLORATION was a mystique for a special breed of people from the start. Over the years who went? People escaping and enforcing the law. Missionaries. Scientists. Military people. Greedy people. Merchants. Whalers. The merely curious. What-

Eskimos at Kotzebue, Alaska, respect their heritage with a local museum. But many arctic artifacts have been carried away.

ever their motives, from the south they came, those men who responded in their own way to the special magnetism of the north. What did they leave behind them in the frigid frontier, and what did they take away, for "contact" was a give-and-take business?

The most obvious things left by explorers were place names and bloodlines. A glance at an arctic map shows *Queen Maud* Gulf, *Peary*land, *Barents* Sea, *Frobisher* Bay, Cape *Dezhnev* and so on, demonstrating the classic early "discoverer" mentality at work, as the men ignored the Native terms and brought fame to themselves, their sponsors, and their friends. Even more important, they left some sturdy descendants making new races in the north: Greenlanders, who are chiefly a mixture of Danes and Inuit; Alaska Natives, almost all of whom have Anglo-Saxon names and bloodlines from whalers; Russian and Norse northerners who inherited some ancestry from the Cossacks and Vikings. The British Hudson's Bay Company, to open fur-trading posts in Canada, sent vigorous young men, mostly Scots, to the northern

68

outposts where they left descendants among the Inuit and the Indians.

The things taken away were legion: artifacts, antiquities, shaman's equipment—American, Canadian, and European museums are full of these things. Explorers also brought back furs, live animals, and the ultimate arctic souvenir, people. Eskimos were caught as if they were wild animals, penned, and taken to Europe as show pieces. They often died en route, but they were of sideshow interest even as cadavers.

The obvious difficulties that faced the first explorers, besides the bad climate, were poor maps, or no maps at all. Some of the ancient charts were deliberate frauds, sold for quick profit when the arctic interest began. Some were filled with previous explorers' mistakes due to mirages and floating islands that were thought to be land. Early geographers believed that there was an open polar sea and that the ice only lay close to the land. One sponsor is said to have directed the captain of an expedition to "go to the North Pole and turn left." The knowledge of the permanent ice pack came much later, as late as the nineteenth century. There was a lack of sensible financial backing, forcing the explorers to lie at times and always to please the sponsor. And as usual among adventurers there was competition, and there were prima donnas seeking personal fame from the start.

Their reasons for going lay in a loose historical pattern. There was always curiosity, to see what was there. Having found a little of what was there, some people went back to get it. The fur trade, fishing, and whaling were early incentives, as well as the search for a passage to the riches of the Orient. When the American continent was discovered it was considered an obstacle blocking the way to the green pastures of Asia! Eventually, scientific interest became a leading reason for heading north, and finally the sport of planting a flag on the geographic North Pole seized the imagination of the world.

The people who went and lived to tell about it shared one thing. *They had to adapt to the Native life-style or they did not survive.* The tragic deaths that filled graves on remote cold shores

Many deaths resulted because arctic explorers insisted on trying to live in European fashion instead of adopting Native life-styles.

were often a result of trying to live a European life in an arctic climate. In spite of historic lessons this still occasionally happens today.

So many heroic men went to the north by so many routes and by such diverse means that whole libraries are filled with books about explorers and their exploits. The first recorded European whose curiosity led him to investigate the mysterious arctic was the Greek navigator Pytheas, who, at about 325 B.C., set out from what is now Marseille, France. According to ancient historians, Pytheas did the incredibly brave act of leaving the safety of the Mediterranean to sail north, leaving Europe behind him to cross the Arctic Circle between Greenland and Scandinavia. He is said to have sailed six days beyond Scotland, reaching a point where the sun barely went below the horizon in summer. He called it "Ultima Thule," a place that has never been positively identified.

Eight hundred years later religion led a group north. Seeking solitude, Ireland's sainted navigator, Brendan, accompanied by eighteen monks, set sail for the north in a large curragh, a hide and frame vessel bearing a strange resemblance to an Eskimo umiak. Brendan is believed to have visited Jan Mayen Island, Iceland, possibly Greenland and other northern lands.

Monsters represent the terrors of unknown regions in 1436 world map.

About 870 the Norse chieftain Ottar, who already lived farther north than any other known European, set out up the Norwegian coast to see how far his land extended. According to the records of King Alfred the Great of England, Ottar passed the North Cape, then sailed east into what are now the White Sea and Barents Sea, finding great walrus ivory.

By A.D. 870, the Vikings, land-hungry Norsemen who went "a-viking," sailing from bay to bay (*vik* to *vik* in Old Norse), began to settle in Iceland. There they found Irish monks who had preceded them by many years. One of the earliest Vikings to arrive, at about A.D. 860, was Floki Vilgerdason, who was reported to have used a raven, that wise old bird of the North, to locate land. Floki passed north of Iceland, near Grimsey Island, probably going above the Arctic Circle, and first settled in the northwest fiords.

Other celebrated Vikings followed into the far north, in the next seven hundred years. The Vikings not only performed incredible feats of seamanship in their open long boats but their adventures were recorded by their literate countrymen. Thanks to the Icelandic sagas, we know intricate details of the lives and fortunes of Eric the Red, who made the first European settlement in Greenland, and his son Leif, who "discovered" America in the year 1000. Their relatives set up colonies in North America, and seem to have made numerous voyages into the arctic. It is be-

Viking ruins at site of colony of Eric the Red in southern Greenland

lieved that the climate was more temperate at that time, allowing
more opportunity to navigate in the northern seas.

In any case, there are numerous remains of Vikings on Baffin,
Ellesmere, and other Canadian islands as well as in Greenland's
arctic area. One saga gives an account of a Viking trading venture
with Eskimos on Baffin Island. At first the Vikings exchanged a
full measure of red cloth for each fur. When the cloth supply ran
low, they tore the measures in half for one fur. Finally they divided and redivided the red cloth until the Natives were receiv-
ing only a narrow strip, but the Vikings still got one fur for each
bit of cloth. The Vikings also brought milk, and the Eskimos liked
it so much that it became the most popular trade item. When the
Eskimos moved their kayaks by flailing their double-ended pad-
dles, the Vikings thought this was a sign of peace!

In 1824, Pelimut, a Native Greenlander, discovered a runic
stone recording a Viking visit near Upernavik, Greenland, at
73°N. To the trained eye, rocky ruins of Viking houses can be
seen throughout the arctic.

The "Little Ice Age," a period of cold weather that lasted roughly from the fourteenth through the sixteenth centuries, slowed down arctic exploration during that time, but the lure of the north was not forgotten.

Meantime the Spanish and the Portuguese were sailing south to establish commerce with China and India. The English and the Dutch, unable to muscle their way into this lucrative trade route, looked again to the north. There must be northern passages to get ships around the troublesome continent of North America, they reasoned. And so was born the great rush for the Northwest and Northeast passages.

The demands of the "civilized" lands of Europe in the middle of the sixteenth century were increasing for the gold, silk, art objects, and furs of the Far East. Daring English and Dutch adventurers found rich merchants and greedly governments to finance them and piratical crews to risk their lives in the ice. By the late 1550's, several enterprising English ships had gone north to the arctic and turned east to Muscovy, or Russia, then ruled by Ivan the Terrible with whom they made a trade arrangement for England. This was the beginning of the Northeast Passage and is now part of the Soviet Northern Sea Route. The Russians had furs that they extracted from their arctic and Siberian Natives as tribute, so the trade with fur-hungry Europe became brisk and lucrative.

Martin Frobisher's monument in the town of Frobisher Bay on Canada's Baffin Island was unveiled in 1976, commemorating that swashbuckling seaman who landed in this spot just south of the Arctic Circle four hundred years ago. Frobisher, who had been in England's Africa trade and had spent some time in prison for alleged acts of piracy, was lured to try to find the Northwest Passage after studying the Zeno map, a document later proved to be false. He made three trips to the arctic, even discovering what he thought was gold but, alas, was only pyrite, or "fool's gold." However, it started the first arctic gold rush, for others tried to follow and get rich. The only result was that his sponsor was jailed for fraud. Frobisher captured some Eskimos and took them

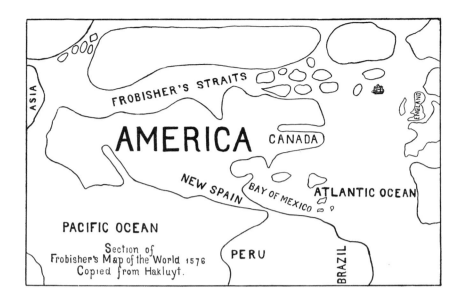

PACIFIC OCEAN

Section of
Frobisher's Map of the World 1576
Copied from Hakluyt.

back to England, feeling that the sight of the Mongoloid Natives would convince the people of England that he had actually reached the Far East. On sailing through a strait with Native people on both shores he was convinced, he said, that he was in the Northwest Passage between Asia and North America.

Frobisher, who became Sir Martin Frobisher, used tricky methods to capture his souvenir Eskimos, which actions aroused the hostility of these "simple" people toward future explorers. On one occasion, he rang a small brass bell over the ship's side to entice interested Eskimos to the ship. When one man approached in great interest, Frobisher dropped the bell into the sea but promptly produced a second one; when the Native came even closer, Frobisher, a powerful man, dropped the bell, seized the Eskimo and kayak, and lifted man and boat aboard his ship. The Eskimo was so distressed that he bit his tongue in two. When Frobisher died in 1594, in a final flamboyant gesture he asked that his heart be cut out and buried in Plymouth, a port from which he had often set out on expeditions, but that his body be buried in London. Of such stuff were Elizabethan explorers made.

A less spectacular man but one with more influence on serious arctic exploration was John Davis. Davis made three voyages into the arctic, 1585–1587, exploring the strait between Greenland and the Canadian islands which now bears his name. He won the friendship of some of the Eskimos by dancing and polar-bear hunting, and when he returned to the same spot later the Eskimos greeted him as an old and trusted friend. Davis was interested in the fish, the flowers, and the animals. He published books that were to have profound influence on later explorers.

Dutchman Willem Barents, who found and charted Spitsbergen and other arctic islands as bases for whaling, was an influential explorer who lost his life in the arctic in 1597. Two hundred and eighty-two years later, Norwegians found Barents' log, weapons, equipment, and religious prints which he had brought for the conversion of the Chinese he had confidently expected to encounter.

Some ships were as famous as their captains. The *Discovery*, a fifty-ton displacement British ship, first went to the arctic in 1601 where the chaplain and the second in command led a mutiny against Captain George Weymouth. Yet they all sailed home together with the mutineers pardoned by Weymouth. Mutinies were common in seas where the captain had no choice but to agree to demands or go into the icy water. Captain Henry Hudson later took the *Discovery* to the arctic, and again there was a mutiny. This time Hudson and his son and a few others were put out in a small boat. They were never seen again. Two of the mutineers who had previously been involved in uprisings against Hudson were eventually punished by fate. Going ashore to pick sorrel, the plant that even today sustains arctic adventurers, they were killed by Natives. The surviving mate, Robert Bylot, took the ship home and was, strangely enough, not punished for the mutiny.

Later Bylot and William Baffin, whose names are on arctic maps, took the *Discovery* back north. Baffin had sailed with Captain James Hall, a man who had achieved a bad name among the Natives in Greenland for his kidnapping crimes. Hall, on a subsequent voyage to the area, was recognized by relatives of the kidnapped person and murdered in revenge. Baffin found and named

Sitka, Alaska, nineteenth-century print

Lancaster Sound but, discouraged at the moment, he returned home, not realizing that this was the entrance to the elusive Northwest Passage.

While the English were gaining control of much of the arctic, the Russians were expanding into Siberia, moving east and north from St. Petersburg in search of furs, much as the Americans moved west a century or so later. They fought the local tribes with the same zeal and destroyed the fur-bearing animals with the same abandon that some Americans did. The merchant family of Stroganovs "rented" Siberia from Ivan the Terrible in 1574, organized a private army of Cossacks, and went after the fur trade with the Natives. The Russians eventually got to the Pacific Ocean and kept right on going east to colonize and kill off more animals and people in Alaska in the eighteenth and nineteenth centuries. They especially went after the sea otters and beavers whose furs were in high fashion in Europe.

Russian explorations of Siberia are among the great blood-and-guts stories of the world of adventure. In 1648, Semeon Ivanovich Dezhnev, a wild Cossack who collected fur tributes for the czar from the Natives in northern Siberia, took a fleet of six small boats down the Kolyma River into the Arctic Ocean, turned east and rounded the jutting cape that now bears his name, went through the strip of water now called the Bering Strait, and reentered Siberia by the Anadyr River. He wrote a semiliterate report of this incredible feat, but it was "filed," never reaching the eyes of the officials in St. Petersburg. Historian G. F. Muller found it in Yakutsk, Siberia, nearly a hundred years later.

Superb horsemen, the Cossacks fought and abused the Natives who sometimes retaliated. Two Cossacks were beheaded and their heads were kept as trophies by the Chuckchi Natives, a warning to other tax collectors.

In London over three hundred years ago the demand for northern furs set in motion an institution that was to make a total

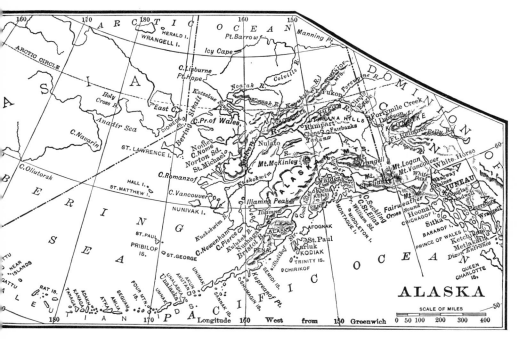

Old map of Alaska

change in the lives of arctic Natives in Canada. King Charles II chartered the "Governor and Company of Adventurers of England Trading into Hudson's Bay," eventually to become known simply as the "Bay." For centuries they traded English goods for furs, establishing a dependence on the western supplies that changed the local culture. The Bay actually governed the Canadian north until quite recent years. As an institution it has declined, but as an historic influence it can never be erased. The Hudson's Bay Company provided some famous arctic explorers for mapping and prospecting. Samuel Hearne explored the Coppermine River with the help of Athapascan Indians. The latters' reward was to be allowed to butcher every Eskimo man, woman, and child at a place now called Bloody Falls. In spite of his connection with this incident in history, Hearne was a brave man and gifted mapper. Alexander Mackenzie, whose company later merged with the Bay, explored the river that bears his name.

While the British were busy in the Canadian arctic, Czar Peter the Great tied up his disorganized Siberian affairs and formed the Great Northern Expedition. Peter did things on a grand scale; his expedition was the largest exploratory operation in polar regions until modern times. Among other missions, Captain Commander Vitus Bering, a Dane in the service of the Russian navy, was instructed to determine if the continents of Asia and North America were separated by water. Bering, after monumental efforts, in 1728 sailed through the strait that now has his name, proving the separation of the continents, but he did not go ashore. (Of course, nobody in charge realized that Cossack Deshnev's filed report had already proved it.) The Russian Northern Expedition mapped large portions of arctic Siberia.

Britain's Captain James Cook went everywhere, including the arctic in 1776. In fact, it was he who named the Bering Strait for that earlier superb navigator he admired, after he passed through the strait on a fair day when he could see Asia on one side and North America on the other. One of Cook's officers on this trip was William Bligh, who was to go down in history as the victim of the mutiny on the *Bounty* some years later.

Cook himself was stabbed in the back and killed by a Hawaiian

Old print shows death of Captain Cook in Hawaii.

Native just after he left the arctic. He was famous, then and now, and his elaborate tomb in Westminster Abbey looks larger than royalty.

In fact, the lives of most of England's famous at about the time of the American Revolution seem to have touched on the arctic one way or another. Footnote on history: A young midshipman from the vessel *Carcass*, operating in the Spitsbergen area, was chased by a polar bear but saved himself by shooting it. This is hardly worth mention except that the midshipman was Horatio Nelson, later England's great hero at the Battle of Trafalgar.

One of the observations that kept recurring in reports of arctic voyages was the presence of whales, enticing vessels to go north, especially to Spitsbergen and Greenland. But whalers were secretive about their voyages for business reasons. Nevertheless, they produced some scientific writings, especially the William Scoresbys, father and son, who made seventeen voyages from England to the arctic between 1803 and 1822. Their maps and journals are still good reading today.

In 1818 exploration took a new turn. The British government offered a reward of twenty thousand pounds to anyone who could find a Northwest Passage to the Orient and five thousand pounds to the first person to reach 89°N. Competition hit a new high. It was an age of great exploration that made the names of Sir John

Barrow (the Second Secretary of the Admiralty who promoted this rash of expeditions), Sir John Ross, Sir William Parry, Sir James Clark Ross, and Sir John Franklin household words in England.

Parry was the most original of these explorers. He left England in 1819 with James Clark Ross (the man who later located the magnetic north pole) as part of the ship's complement. Parry was the first explorer to go with plans to spend the winter, rather than merely make a summer foray. He kept his men healthy and comfortable, with such innovations as using the ship's heat pipes to grow mustard and cress to prevent scurvy, a disease caused by lack of Vitamin C. The morale was kept high with writing and performing "theatricals," and a weekly newspaper, the first in the arctic. Called *The North Georgia Gazette*, it lasted a year and a half in 1819–1820. The men did not find the Northwest Passage, but they explored Melville Island with a jury-rigged wagon whose tracks were still visible thirty years later. On another expedition Parry tried to reach the North Pole, with reindeer hauling the provision sledges over the ice. Men took over the hauling after they ate the reindeer. He gave up when he realized that the ice drift south was greater than their daily push to the north!

Sir John Franklin also went to the arctic in 1819, but his orders were to make land explorations and survey the coast east of Canada's Coppermine River, as Hearne had done earlier. His exploits of bravery and harrowing adventures are sometimes forgotten in the light of later developments in Franklin's career. On his third and final trip north seeking the Northwest Passage, his two ships, the *Erebus* and the *Terror*, were supposed to winter over. In 1845 Franklin was an old man of fifty-nine, famous and experienced. Yet this expedition is a classic saga of snobbery— how *not* to travel in the arctic. Franklin, born the son of a modest shopkeeper, had developed a taste for high living. On his ships, officers tried to live like British upper class.

Although the outside world did not know it, Franklin died in June, 1847, following the deaths of nine of his officers and fifteen men, probably from scurvy. Native people got their life-sustain-

Old print shows sailing vessel ramming an iceberg.

ing vitamins from animal organs. Franklin had employed professional hunters, required the men to carry greater loads than officers, used heavy ammunition to shoot birds (the gentleman's sport), and carried formal attire and silverware so that no detail of social graces would be lost in the northern wilds. But he never took a look at how the Natives lived.

When no word of Franklin's expedition had been heard by 1848, three years after the party left England, the Admiralty sponsored a massive search for Franklin. In all there were forty-two expeditions launched from many nations to try to find the missing, filling the mid-century presses of the world. Finally Dr. John Rae, a highly competent arctic traveler and surveyor who had learned to live like the Eskimos, in 1851 picked up some wreckage that seemed to be from Franklin's ship. Two years later he purchased a gilt naval officer's cap band from an Eskimo, and he heard many odd stories of strange white men from the Eskimos whose language he had mastered. He turned up initialed spoons and forks, Franklin's Hanoverian Order of Merit medal (just the thing needed in the arctic!) and stories of cannibalism. As the fragments of the tragedy emerged it seemed that Franklin's ships had sailed into the polar ice pack, due to faulty maps rather than poor judgment, and were finally caught fast in ice in 1846, never to be released. With Franklin dead and no prospects of relief, in April, 1848, the 105 remaining men set forth ill and unprepared on ice, apparently taking most of their personal pos-

Old map of Canada

sessions with them, things that were abandoned to give clues of the march that was equally marked by dead bodies, for they all perished.

When Rae made an orderly report of the tragedy from the evidence he had uncovered, it set up a furor of disbelief. Rae was assailed for mentioning that any of Britain's finest could have been involved in cannibalism. Charles Dickens, of all people, rose to Rae's defense.

Meantime the arctic was crowded with expeditions there to prove Rae wrong and to find the missing men. Franklin's widow raised a sum of money and sent the yacht *Fox*, commanded by Leopold McClintock, to search. She herself went to Alaska, shortly after the United States purchased it from Russia in 1867, looking for information. Even today there are papers and souvenirs from Franklin's party turning up, sometimes anonymously placed by Natives on the desks of officials or librarians.

Among the Franklin effects turned up by McClintock were skeletons, cairn messages, a ship's boat and a sledge with an estimated 1400 pounds of food, cutlery, tools, and toilet articles. The first skeleton he found, in May, 1859, was that of a steward, in uniform, still carrying a clothes brush.

Americans were fascinated with the Franklin searches. One of the most noteworthy was Charles Francis Hall, a printer from Cincinnati, Ohio, who managed to raise money for a Franklin search in 1860. Hall was one of the new breed of explorers who found that it was important to learn from the Natives. He studied

Ship approaches the Muir Glacier, Alaska.

Sailors procuring fresh water from an iceberg

the language and had respect for the Natives in his three trips to the arctic. He died mysteriously in Greenland in 1871. Chauncey Loomis, a Dartmouth professor with an insatiable curiosity, went himself in 1968 to investigate this unsolved cause of death and discovered that Hall had died of arsenic poisoning, quite likely at the hand of someone on the ship.

The search for Franklin finally lost its lure (except in the arctic where it still lives on in legends today), but new interests brought a new kind of explorer into the limelight. A German, Lieutenant Karl Weyprecht, had an idea for establishing a series of weather stations around the arctic to learn more about the earth's magnetism. He died before his plan was carried out, but in 1882 ten nations did arrange this. A team from the United States Army, suffering horrible hardships, maintained a station about eight degrees from the North Pole for three years under the command of Lieutenant Adolphus Greely. Most of the party died, due to the failure of relief ships to arrive, but Greely and the other survivors returned with the scientific material, great heroes. By combining their findings with those of other nations, a great deal of useful information was added to the world's geography.

The Northeast Passage, which is actually today's Soviet Northern Sea Route, never captured the public imagination to the extent that the Northwest Passage did. However, explorers did go after it. Baron Nils Adolf Erik Nordenskjöld, a Swedish university professor and veteran arctic explorer, accomplished it in 1879.

That same year American George DeLong, Lieutenant, USN, sailed from San Francisco for the North Pole in the *Jeanette*. The ship was crushed in ice and the captain and most of the crew perished. Newspaper accounts of the tragedy were seen by a young Norwegian doctor, Fridtjof Nansen. He was highly intrigued later by stories of the strange appearance in the next few years of wreckage of the *Jeanette* on the southwest coast of Greenland. There must be orderly currents and drifts in the Arctic Ocean, he reasoned, and he determined to experiment with this idea.

In 1888 Nansen had been the first European to cross the Greenland ice cap. He was able to get backing for a specially reinforced ship of original design, the *Fram*, which he allowed to be frozen into the pack ice in 1893. Its movement for the next three years with the ice proved his theory of polar drift from west to east. Another of his ideas was the "Nansen bottle" with which he took ocean samples that taught scientists much about the earth and the seas. Nansen, considered the father of oceanography, left the *Fram* in the polar ice under the command of Otto Sverdrup and, with one companion, set out by dogsled to look for the North Pole. They did not reach it but Nansen concluded that the Pole lay under the shifting ice pack. Today the sturdy *Fram* sits in a museum in Oslo, Norway.

There had been so many searches for the Northwest Passage, searches for Franklin, and searches for Franklin's searchers that the public began to get tired of it all. It was in this atmosphere that the tough, shrewd Norwegian Roald Amundsen, who is much more famous as an Antarctic explorer, finally made the first successful voyage through the Northwest Passage. It took three hard years in his little ship the *Gjoa*, and it ended without much fanfare in Nome, Alaska, in 1906. Meantime, Nansen had planted the idea that luck and good mathematical instruments would enable a person to find the exact geographic North Pole, a thought that developed into a new arctic sport.

Polar madness went into high gear with the arctic star, Robert

E. Peary, of the United States Navy. Like others who got infected from reading a book, young Peary, while on duty as a junior officer surveying a route for a proposed canal across Nicaragua, read Baron Nordenskjöld's book on Greenland. A passion seized him to become the first white man to reach the North Pole, and between 1886 and 1909 Peary, obsessed with his goal, made eight arctic trips. The idea of arctic "firsts" caused an insidious itch in explorers and their sponsors, for sponsors they had to have. Explorers had to perfrom daring deeds to entice lecture-ticket purchasers, money from rich armchair travelers, and organizations with cash to spare for worthy ventures. Peary on each trip had to make or claim some new accomplishment. On April 6, 1909, when he finally reached the North Pole, or its vicinity (he never had to support his claim), he was carrying the flags of the United States, his fraternity at Bowdoin College, the Daughters of the American Revolution, and the Navy League, as well as a few other pieces of "damn foolishness" that equaled Franklin's silver plates and medals. He is reported to have said "Mine at last," and to have "presented the North Pole to President Theodore Roosevelt." His detractors were critical of his arrogance and ego. He was careful to be the only white man in the final group, which consisted of Peary, his black servant Matthew Henson, and four Eskimos. By prearrangement the support team, headed by Captain Robert Bartlett, had been sent back to the ship just short of the destination so Peary's personal glory would be unshared.

Did Peary actually reach the Pole? Many people wondered if he knew his exact position with only some pages torn from the *Nautical Almanac* and a sextant and a chronometer for finding out where he was. He had to have the sun's elevation the same in the four quadrants to be sure he was at 90°N, where north, east, south, and west converge. That is difficult, a nearly impossible feat, according to experienced navigators. He made incredible speed in returning from his April 7 triumph, for on April 23 he was back at his base in Greenland, having averaged twenty-six miles a day from the Pole. Later, when his ship reached Labrador, he sent off a message, "Stars and Stripes Nailed to the Pole."

But the blow fell when he discovered that five days earlier Dr.

Frederick Cook had telegraphed from the Shetland Islands that he had reached the North Pole in April, 1908, a year before Peary. Peary returned to a world which had acclaimed Cook as the hero of the hour, the first white man at the North Pole. Peary accused Cook of being a fraud and a liar, but Cook did not respond in kind. However, various learned committees seemed to concur that Peary was the only man who had actually been at the North Pole, even though he continued to be the victim of many insults. The National Geographic Society, one of Peary's supporters, accepted his claim, and Peary has gone down in history as the first white man at the North Pole, for whatever that is worth. Cook was always suspect as he had earlier made a highly questionable claim to having reached the summit of Mount McKinley.

The Peary/Cook fight was meat for the press of the world for a long time, and it has still not been laid to rest. Peary has been accused by his detractors of many misdeeds—one that he illegally took three ancient meteorites from Greenland and sold them for personal profit. This is not true. He located and removed the meteorites with the help of friendly Eskimos, and at great risk to himself, and gave them to the American Museum of Natural History in New York City, where they can be seen today. Peary made himself a controversial character, but despite his personality problems he remains in retrospect a determined, single-minded, physically brave (his toes were frozen off!) explorer who acted according to the customs of the period. Maybe Cook and Peary both reached the Pole, maybe neither did. But the fanfare of the quest for the North Pole had peaked, and a new breed of arctic explorer took over.

Vilhjalmur Stefansson, born in Canada of Icelandic parents, was an American citizen. An anthropologist, he was trained in African studies, when an unexpected offer came his way. Due to his Norse ancestry he had an interest in Vikings and had done a scholarly paper on their North American settlements which caught the attention of an arctic expedition leader. Poised on his way to Africa, he was invited to join the arctic venture. When he accepted this challenge in 1906 he was to establish himself as one of the greatest arctic experts of all times. He spent much of the

Summer at Thule Air Force Base in Greenland

rest of his life in the north, chiefly in the Canadian arctic. He learned to live as an Eskimo, even making his own skin garments. He wrote, lectured, taught, and interpreted, freely sharing his findings. He was so at home in the north that he was brash enough to call it "the friendly arctic." His *Arctic Manual* was the standard book of reference issued to American military in the arctic in World War II.

Yet he, too, was controversial. During his expedition in the vessel *Karluk* (1913–1918), he left the ship under the command of Captain Robert Bartlett (the same one who had gone almost to the Pole with Peary) after the ship became stuck in ice. While Stefansson was proceeding on his dog-team expedition, the ship was crushed. Bartlett got most of the ship's company to safety, but lives were lost and criticism of Stefansson surfaced from some of the survivors.

Stefansson is credited with originating the idea of using a base camp on floating ice for meteorological and oceanographic observations.

Knud Rasmussen, an educated Greenlander, another of the new breed of explorers, was unique in that he himself was part Eskimo. After setting up a trading post with Peter Freuchen near the present Thule Air Base in Greenland, he made five arctic expeditions by dogsled between 1912 and 1924, mapping and studying as he traveled from Greenland to Siberia, trying to gain more knowledge of the Native people and their origins.

By the 1920's the arctic was being explored from the air. Lieutenant Commander, later Admiral, Richard E. Byrd made the first polar crossing through the air on May 9, 1926, his position verified by the latest air navigational instruments. There had been earlier unsuccessful air attempts made by, among others, Roald Amundsen and an American, Lincoln Ellsworth. Two days after Byrd's successful flight, Italian General Umberto Nobile, Amund-

Norwegian children play below the statue of Roald Amundsen, Norwegian explorer.

Lincoln Ellsworth, polar explorer

sen, and Ellsworth crossed the pole in the dirigible *Norge*. Two years later in 1928 General Nobile set out again in an airship, the *Italia*. He reached the Pole, but crashed the next day. In the search for Nobile, who was rescued, the veteran explorer Amundsen was lost and never found.

The Soviets made a number of early flights off the Siberian coast. In 1934 when an exploring party headed by Otto Schmidt was set adrift on an ice floe far from shore after their ship was crushed, Soviet flyers rescued all of them by landing on the ice. In 1937, Schmidt headed an air expedition that landed Ivan Papanin and three others in the North Pole area to carry out observations on the first drifting ice research station. They called it North Pole 1, the first of many such North Pole drifting stations with successive numbers. Prepared for winter, the Soviets set up comfortable, radio-equipped quarters on the drifting ice. The camp was later removed and rebuilt for display at the Arctic Museum in Leningrad.

One of the last great exploratory polar journeys was made by four men with sledges and dog teams, under the leadership of Englishman Wally Herbert, in the British Trans-Arctic Expedition of 1968–1969, from Point Barrow, Alaska, to Spitsbergen via the North Pole, a journey of 3,620 miles, in 464 days. Herbert has described, in his book, the difficulties, even in this day and age with present instruments, of locating, exactly, the North Pole; he did as Peary did, shot solar sights, and crisscrossed the area to be sure he had been there. There were, however, shore stations tracking his progress, as well as support aircraft dropping supplies, and verifying his positions and track.

Earlier, Ralph Plaisted, a snowmobile enthusiast from Minnesota, for an advertising gimmick as well as an adventure, tried to reach the North Pole by snowmobile in 1967, but was prevented by ice breakup. Plaisted tried again in 1968 and succeeded, becoming the first man since Peary to reach the Pole on the surface ice. In 1971, an Italian expedition using dog teams also reached the Pole.

Naomi Uemura, a 37-year-old Japanese explorer, became the first person known to reach the exact North Pole, alone, by dog team, in late April, 1978. Uemura was already legendary in the high arctic when he departed in March from Ellesmere Island on his 600-mile trek over the polar ice, for he had worked for years in mountain climbing, skiing, and canoeing in high latitudes. After a dangerous encounter with a polar bear that tore the tent and ate the dog food, Uemura shot and ate the bear. He was tracked by meteorological satellite NIMBUS SIX which passes over the Pole every 108 minutes, and his position was accurately pinpointed when he reach his goal. He, and other Japanese, plan more arctic adventures.

With all the sophisticated electronic aids to exploration available today it might seem that the romantic days of arctic exploration are over. But the mystique won't die even though it is possible now for a tourist to fly to the North Pole by merely

Crew of the nuclear-powered submarine USS Queenfish *at the North Pole*

paying the charter air fare. Submarines under the ice still hold a challenge. When in August, 1958, the United States Navy atomic-powered submarine *Nautilus* under the command of Commander William R. Anderson passed under the ice at the North Pole the world was seized with arctic underwater excitement.

Less than a year later in March, 1959, the USS *Skate*, another atomic submarine, not only went under the ice but broke through it at the exact North Pole. When Commander James Calvert and his men emerged to walk on the ice they carried with them a small urn containing the ashes of Sir Hubert Wilkins, an Australian who had explored the arctic by ice, air, and sea. Wilkins had, in 1931, rented an old American submarine for five dollars a year and made an effort, unsuccessful, to sail the old tub under the ice. A solemn service was held for Sir Hubert who had at last attained the Pole. It was an international gesture that seemed to

Scuba divers from the crew of the USS Queenfish *prepare for a swim under the arctic ice.*

Seagulls on the icebergs are the souls of departed explorers.

unite all brave arctic adventurers past and future.

Of course, the souls of arctic explorers stay within the Circle. How else to account for all the sea gulls perched on icebergs there? Everyone knows they are the souls of the departed explorers.

8

Resources, Transportation, and Tourism

++

We broke camp, and, struggling with our packs, we hiked to the weathered, overcrowded terminal building at Resolute's busy airport in Canada. We were hoping to get space on a Twin Otter bush plane to take us farther north.

Two enormous commercial jets had landed a few minutes before, spilling out their passengers who had come north to work, exploit, preach, teach, see, study, and who knows what.

The Arctic's rich resources lay behind it all, we decided, for the mineral wealth had forced sophisticated transportation for workers. With the transportation available, tourists were coming, too.

The most unlikely lot of lookers was a tour party of little old ladies, literally in tennis shoes. They were walking single file, clutching their bird glasses, ready to take on a two-day arctic visit. Polar bears we had expected, but nothing on our ceiling map had prepared us for this.

++

ANYONE WHO has seethed in line for gasoline, only to find the pump empty, or has shivered during a winter electric-power outage, has thought with longing of the much discussed oil in the north. People speak with rage, awe, and hope of the arctic oil which has long been known. There are ancient Eskimo folktales

95

Old print of polar bear on the ice

of naughty children who play in puddles of it and diaries of nineteenth-century travelers who complain of getting "tar" on their boots. Not only is there oil within the Circle, but there are enough other resources to make corporations compete to manipulate governments for mineral leases and transportation rights in the get-rich frontier.

The suspected arctic riches influenced Secretary of State William H. Seward to push through the purchase of Alaska from Russia immediately after the American Civil War. He saw the arctic as a potentially strategic military area, and he and his fol-

Old print: "An Arctic Scene"

lowers tried to persuade Congress to attempt to purchase Greenland and Iceland as well, a project that had no success from any of the concerned parties. When the Western Union Telegraph Company tried to lay a cable across the Bering Strait to connect North America and Europe at about this time (the project was abandoned when a cable was successfully taken across the Atlantic), the voluminous journals of the scientific corps of the company laid a foundation for arctic natural history and mineral studies.

Minerals are not the only natural resources in high latitudes. There is fresh water, with enough of it stored in glaciers for parched throats everywhere. And then there are animals.

The Eskimos or Inuit, Indians, Chuckchis, Lapps, Evenks, and other ancient people of the north survived on whales, fish, seals, walrus, caribou, reindeer, musk-oxen, polar bear, and other creatures that gave man meat, heat, tools, boat-building supplies, and housing material. To add to these local riches there were dogs for pulling the bone-and-skin sleds. Arctic animals are still economically valuable today, but they are not as important as the ever growing mineral developments.

Oil and gas head the list. They are present in Alaska, Greenland, Canada, Scandinavia, the Soviet Union, and the arctic islands, not only on land but under the seas and glaciers. It is

Reindeer in Lapland, old print

Alyeska pipeline crosses Yukon River in Alaska.

probably an exaggeration, but a Soviet news story states that the arctic region of the USSR is sitting in a bowl of oil. Nobody can measure the quantity of hydrocarbons within the Arctic Circle; yet it is not renewable, bringing up the question of whether it is worthwhile to disrupt and destroy people, land, and animals to get out a substance that, once removed, is gone for good.

In the late 1970's there were active drilling and exploration at Prudhoe Bay, Alaska; Holsteinborg, Greenland; in the Mackenzie River Delta, Bathurst, Axel Heiberg, Banks, and Victoria Island in Canada; in Norway's Lofoten Islands and her protectorate Spitsbergen; and, by various nations, in the Kara, Barents, Beaufort, Chuckchi, and Norwegian Seas. The only positive way to know the presence of oil is to drill a well, but it is possible through geologic processes to locate the possibility of a reservoir. Environmentalists throughout the world are alert to the inherent dangers of these ventures. In 1978 there were 248 petroleum leases within the Arctic Circle.

The continuing discovery of gold below the Circle in the Yukon and Alaska in the last half of the nineteenth century inspired prospectors to keep moving north. Gold had already been found in arctic Siberia, and it was no surprise eventually to find that there were gold deposits throughout the north. There is iron ore in substantial quantity too. Probably the best of the old and continuously worked sites are at Kiruna in Sweden.

Add to that, copper, lead, and zinc in great amounts. Early in the 1900's it was known that there was copper on Canada's Victoria Island. In Alaska, early geologists found quantities of copper among other valuable ores, but there was no means then of turning these potential riches into pay dirt. Today rich lead and zinc workers (who are not paid in pennies!) from the new Strathcona mines at Nansivik, near Pond Inlet, Canada, fill the airport at Resolute on Cornwallis Island, waiting for planes to take them "outside" where they can spend their high wages.

As for coal, even before 1800 when sail-powered whaling vessels went into the Arctic Ocean, whalers found veins of coal on the surface north of Bering Strait in Alaska. They gathered this for heating their cold wooden ships. Later, in the mid-nineteenth century when arctic whaling was at its height, steam-powered vessels used the coal for power. (The first steam-powered ship to go into the arctic was the *Victory* in 1829 under Captain John Ross.)

Active coal mines on Spitsbergen, with new ones being devel-

Coal operations in Spitsbergen

Coal is carried in overhead cars from Spitsbergen mines to ships.

oped, today bring two thousand Norwegian miners and their families to this small arctic island, where workers, including the teachers in the modern school at Longyearbyen, have tax benefits as well as a tightly knit social life that keeps them together year after year. Two other coal mining districts on the island are Barentsburg and Pyramiden, both manned by Soviet workers. There are only formal communications between the two nations represented on this island; the Soviets are there by treaty, and the two colonies see little of each other.

Appropriate jewels in the crown of the world are the diamonds found in Siberia and the mountain of jade on the Kobuk River in Alaska. There are deposits of silver, chromium, and platinum as well.

Greenland alone has identified, besides the hydrocarbons, copper, iron, lead, zinc, molybdenum, chromium, nickel, graphite, asbestos, limestone, granite, soapstone, cryolite, and many more in this largely unexplored land.

The Soviet Union, which probably has more arctic riches then the rest of the world, is pushing hard to develop its resources. Nickel has long been mined on the Kola Peninsula near the Norwegian border, and there are vast supplies of phosphorus, tungsten, vermiculite, potash, and mica. At Norilsk in Siberia, hydrides of lithium, used for rocket fuel, are a well-guarded commodity. An important mineral that passes through the port of Murmansk is apatite, called the "stone of fertility" because it is used in the manufacture of fertilizers that make high agricultural yields in otherwise poor soils.

Soviets launch a meteorological rocket M-100 from Heis Island (Franz Josef Land).

These are only some of the known arctic minerals; think of what is yet to be discovered. But knowing they are there is only an academic exercise: to mine and market them is another thing. Mining and refining take energy, and getting the goods to population centers takes carriers that can combat the challenging climate. Yet it would seem that, with all the wind and waterfalls available in the arctic, the power potential is there.

Despite the problems of construction, including special concrete for subfreezing weather, frozen fingers, short supplies, and the everlasting permafrost, a hydroelectric plant was built in the arctic as early as 1930 on the Kola Peninsula. This was the first of many great hydroelectric installations in the Soviet Union. There was some cooperation with neighboring Norway and Finland on these projects. A Finnish firm which built one of the dams hewed out an underground powerhouse ninety meters long and forty meters high in solid granite. The water flows through tunnels in the granite to power the turbines.

The first European transportation into the arctic was by ship, and maritime shipping continues today in spite of the long months of frozen waterways.

Modern icebreakers have made it possible to increase the shipping period so that supply vessels can get to small settlements which have no suitable airports. Icebreakers are rough and tough ships with bows designed to cut ice. They have a quickly transferable liquid ballast that enables the ship to move up and down, and side to side, lurching and smashing the top of the ice to break it and push it aside, creating a channel so that other ships can follow in a convoy.

The most famous of the regular arctic convoys are the ones which operate in the Soviet Northern Sea Route from Murmansk through Bering Strait to Vladivostok, a trip that can now be done in twenty-eight days. This is the Northeast Passage, so long sought by early explorers and developed by the new Soviet government since 1920. After World War II even more attention was paid to this shipping lane which with the aid of icebreakers is open five months of the year to take supplies into and raw materials out of the interior. Hydrofoils and barges bringing raw

Hudson's Bay Company fills grocery orders for Inuit patrons after ship unloads in Canadian arctic.

materials to the mouths of the Ob, Lena, and Yenesei Rivers contribute to the efficiency of the sea operations, which are often led by the atomic icebreakers *Arktika, Lenin,* and *Sibir.*

The Soviets have tried other ice removal techniques such as salting, blasting, and spreading coal dust, but icebreakers remain the most efficient sea-ice weapons.

Canadian icebreakers have had some heroic tasks in the treacherous waters of their archipelago. The *St. Roch,* a sturdy little ship in the service of the Royal Canadian Mounted Police, made the first west-to-east trip through the Northwest Passage in 1940, and then made the return trip from Halifax to Vancouver.

Supply ships that service arctic communities in Canada and Alaska in the summer months often anchor out and the freight is brought in by barge. The local people turn out to help, around the clock. Children stay up all night in the holiday atmosphere, as toys and TVs, candy bars, blue jeans, building supplies, and new

snowmobiles are brought ashore to be whisked to the warehouse of the local trading post or cooperative store.

Greenland's west coast is serviced in summer by a fleet of small freighter-passenger ships. In Norway similar ships can operate throughout the year in many places. In the fiord country there are hundreds of ferries to link islands to the daily coastal express ship

LEFT: *Busy Greenlandic harbor*

RIGHT: *Greenlander oper- ates small ship.*

BELOW LEFT: *Fishing boats in Grimsey Island harbor in Iceland's arctic*

BELOW: *Children steal a ride on tractor, one of the few local vehicles, to meet plane on Iceland's Grimsey Island.*

service in the busy ice-free harbors.

There is even a small Icelandic ship that carries freight and passengers from Akureyri to the arctic island of Grimsey most of the year.

Rivers that empty into the Arctic Ocean are busy freight routes. In addition to the Soviet rivers, the broad, muddy

ABOVE AND BELOW: S.S. Manhattan *in arctic ice*

Canadian Mackenzie River is one of the great highways to the arctic, bringing barges filled with houses, machinery, and food, and returning with raw materials from the remote areas.

A shipping experiment that didn't work in Canada's arctic waters, that cost $39 million, and nearly put the United States into a bad diplomatic situation with her neighbor, was the incident of the *Manhattan*, a heavy-duty tanker with special reinforcements for ice. The American Humble Oil Company took this monster through the Northwest Passage in 1969; oil was gushing at Prudhoe, Alaska, and if a tanker could get through the tortuous Canadian passage then Humble could deliver it profitably to East Coast markets.

Residents of Resolute on Cornwallis Island were amazed, and Canadians were enraged, when the 150,000-ton tanker appeared in the harbor there with United States Coast Guard helicopters flying overhead, only to move on westward without consulting anyone. Canada had always regarded the Northwest Passage as her inland waters, although the United States and other nations, if they thought of it at all, considered it the high seas. The status was now to be put to the test. Arctic watchers were not altogether surprised that the tanker got hopelessly stuck in the six- to eight-foot ice in McClure Strait. This hazardous route was chosen because it was, at that time, outside the then Canadian three-mile limit and was therefore, by *Manhattan* standards, the high seas. (Canada now enforces a twelve-mile limit.)

It took Canada's strongest new icebreaker—Canada has pioneered in sturdy icebreakers—to dislodge the tanker and lead it to Prudhoe Bay through the narrow Prince of Wales Strait. The Canadian government took swift action to restrict tankers by passing strong environmental laws to be observed in her delicate waters where oil spillage would do damage never before considered.

What about getting the oil out by commercial submarines? In

Nuclear-powered submarine USS Hammerhead *on the surface at the Pole*

that way a tanker could go under the water, a jurisdictional teaser that has not yet been tested, either for efficiency or legality, but it lurks there as a possiblity. It has been proved that military submarines can indeed operate under the ice of the Arctic Ocean.

Alaska's Prudhoe oil finally got to market by pipeline. Pipelines are not new in the north. Alaska had them operating during World War II to supply military stations, and other arctic countries have used pipelines of one sort or another for years. One advanced idea is tunneling—that is, to dig a tunnel to protect a pipeline under water or land. Tunnels beneath the sea would not disturb the ice and there would be minimum environmental damage to land. This has not been tested, but it is under consideration on drawing boards now, especially in Canada, where this might prove the only effective way of getting the oil and gas from rich but frozen islands.

This idea suggests another new thought, that of using pipelines and tunnels to remove ores and minerals by the "slurry" method. Slurry is simply a suspension of liquid in water, and if minerals such as iron ore could be mixed with antifreeze and liquid they could be piped to a processing center in the south.

Railroads in the arctic are another means of getting the minerals out. Sweden and Norway had a railroad line above the Arctic Circle by the middle of the nineteenth century to take iron ore from the Swedish mines to the Norwegian seaport of Narvik, one of the world's major ore-shipping ports. It is kept ice free by a current from the Gulf Stream. This railroad was electrified in 1922 and has for years carried energetic hikers and tourists to the fiord country of Norway along with its ore loads. Norway has another arctic railroad that goes above the Circle to Bodo.

Before the 1917 Revolution, Imperial Russia had built a railroad almost to the Arctic Circle connecting Moscow with Archangel on the White Sea. Later the new Soviet government built an arctic railroad connecting this line with Khal'Mer Yu, near the Kara Sea. In 1916 the last Czar, needing supplies as war and revolution closed in upon his country, began construction of a railroad and new sea terminal on the Arctic Ocean. Running

Rail and ship commerce in Murmansk

from St. Petersburg (now Leningrad) to the new town of Murmansk, the project was taken over by the Soviet government in 1917 and made an important naval and commercial activity.

Now Murmansk is the arctic's largest commercial city with a population of 360,000. In 1975 alone nine million tons of cargo went through its port, which is ice free due to ocean currents. The railroad to Murmansk was later extended west to transport nickel from the mines near the Norwegian and Finnish borders. Murmansk is known to many American servicemen and merchant mariners as the end of the "Murmansk run," a highly hazardous ship convoy route that carried supplies to the Soviets who were fighting Nazi Germany in World War II.

Other than the terminal lines of a railroad that connects Dudenka and Norilsk to the Trans-Siberian Railroad and a few minor shuttles, there are no other railroads above the Arctic Circle in the USSR or elsewhere. When Canada and the United States were undergoing tantrums of indecision about how to get oil and gas out of the arctic about 1970, railroads were considered in North America. But nothing came of it after the Alyeska pipeline from Prudhoe Bay to Valdez in Alaska was decided upon.

Buses carry passengers to remote areas in Lapland.

Road building is difficult in the far north, but roads exist. Lapland is easily accessible now by Scandinavia's fine year-round highway system which regularly takes trucks, buses, and cars to Europe's arctic. In Canada the well-graveled Dempster Highway, built with oil in mind, begins at Dawson in the Yukon and when completed will go to Inuvik on the Mackenzie River and eventually on to Tuktoyaktuk on the Arctic Ocean. This road connects

Traffic control post on controversial haul road in Alaskan arctic

with the Alaska Highway which will make it technically possible to drive from anywhere in the United States or Canada to the Arctic Ocean.

The rest of the arctic is virtually without roads with the exception of some short truck routes in the Soviet Union. There is a proposal for a trans-Siberian highway for heavy truck transport, but there are relatively so few private automobiles in the USSR that a highway system is hardly a consideration there.

One of the most controversial roads in the north is the hastily constructed "haul road" from Fairbanks to Prudhoe Bay in Alaska, built for trucks to service the Aleyska pipeline construction. When the road turned into a sea of mud as summer came it proved conclusively that permafrost was the natural enemy of arctic roads.

However, the controversy was mostly due to the stipulation that the road would not be open to general public use. A number of people exploded at this ruling. One group believed that if the public were allowed to drive vacation vehicles to the Arctic

German tourists disembark from Greenland vessel for a day of mountain fishing and hiking.

*Inuit ranger and friends at
Auyuittuq National Park
on Canada's Baffin Island*

Ocean that Native people and wildlife would be disturbed. It might cause a strip development through the Brooks Range, cutting at the heart of some of the earth's last wild land. Others felt their rights were being violated in not being permitted the free use of an existing road, the access to which was tax funded. In 1978 the haul road remains closed to public traffic with guards posted to keep out casual travelers.

Ice roads are another matter. They have long been one of the most efficient ways of getting around in the north. A thickly frozen river or lake can give a smooth surface for winter travel, and heavy ice provides natural bridges. Of course, these collapse if they get much heat. Along Soviet rivers a solution is to make a rough clearing by the river's edge and pack it with snow to make a firm foundation. Then when the river breaks up there is still a road for vehicles.

A bizarre proposition was made to United States Senator Warren Magnussen, chairman of the Alaska International Rail and Highway Commission, that a highway might be built across Alaska to the Bering Strait and a bridge or tunnel constructed to cross the fifty-mile span of water to the Soviet Union. It was suggested that atomic-powered trains could take freight and passengers under the water to Siberia and link up with the Trans-Siberian Railroad to Europe. Apparently this was scrapped as science fiction, although there are congressional records of the idea.

All vehicles don't need roads. In most arctic villages, with the exception of the Soviet Union, in winter and summer snappy trail bikes and snow machines endlessly fill the limited village streets and surrounding country, with or without snow. But despite stories that the snowmobile has replaced reindeer and dog travel in the north, there is a trend now to return to the animals for secure overland treks. As some Inuit and Samer people put it, a dead snow machine won't keep you warm, find its way home, or provide food in the face of starvation. In Greenland there are restrictions on snow machines. They are permitted, but they may not be used for hunting. This has kept the dog teams going and has cut down on the gas-consuming snow machines, which can only have social use.

Too many fatal accidents in snowmobiles and too much environmental damage done by all-terrain vehicles such as cat trains, snow tractors, and the like are making people look in new directions for arctic transportation. One solution may be the hovercraft air cushion vehicles which do little damage to the delicate arctic earth. Hovercraft find frozen rivers an ideal road, and even pressure ridges are no obstacle. However, hovercraft are found to be a menace to some animals and nesting birds.

Ultimately aircraft is the answer to arctic transportation for most people and small necessities. From terrifyingly small single-engine bush charter planes to twin-engined toll flights (where the plane flies only when there is a full load) even the most remote

LEFT: *Busy scene at Green-landic airport.*

BELOW: *Greenlandic children return from holi-day in Denmark.*

BOTTOM LEFT: *Inuit family waits for toll flight.*

BOTTOM LEFT: *Passenger waiting room at airlines terminal building at Point Hope, Alaska.*

ABOVE: *Charter flights will take you anywhere in the arctic—for a price.*

RIGHT: *Airport scene, Canadian arctic.*

BELOW: *Airlines fly a toll service, when the plane is full, to Grise Fiord on Canada's Ellesmere Island.*

Hikers wait for train in national park in Sweden.

villages can be serviced—for a price. Overhead, larger jets fly circumpolar routes, and internal scheduled jet service covers most of the north now. In Greenland where the ice cap makes landing strips hard to build, scheduled helicopter service can quickly move people from remote districts to the international airports at Sondre Stromfjord and Narssarssuaq for quick transportation to Europe. There is no direct scheduled transportation of any sort between Greenland and the United States, nor between Alaska and the Soviet Union, which, when one looks at the map of the crown of the world, seems an astonishing situation in these days of easy flying. From some parts of Alaska people can see Siberia on the horizon, yet there is no ship or plane to carry freight or people from one shore to the other. To get to Siberia from Alaska a passenger must fly from Anchorage, Alaska, to Tokyo, Japan, and then go by ship or plane to Siberia—a long journey for a short distance.

The opening up of minerals and transportation in the Arctic

Circle has built up a new by-product resource—tourism. There are national parks in the Scandinavian arctic where trains and buses or private automobiles can easily get backpackers into the wilds. There are canoeists and kayakers on Alaskan, Canadian, Greenland, and even Spitsbergen streams.

Fancy tourist ships take well-heeled tourists to the North Cape in Norway and spill them out to fill cosmopolitan hotels in arctic towns. Elegant cruise ships of many nations, including Soviet vessels, appear in the harbors of Tromsö and Hammerfest in Norway, and even in Spitsbergen's Longyearbyen, among other arctic ports of call. Especially among Europeans, arctic ship trips are *in*.

Most of the Native people are quick to use the opportunity to sell souvenirs, perform folk dances, or offer a taxi ride, often on the town's only road to the town's only hotel. But there are opportunities for rewarding tourist experiences, such as the museum in Kotzebue, Alaska, where NANA, the Northwest Alaska Native Association, has built a museum of Inuit culture that can give a

Tromsö, Norway, an arctic city

Soviet tourists gaze at the arctic city of Tromsö, Norway, from their cruise ship.

Norwegian and Soviet passenger ships at Long-yearbyen, Spitsbergen

Soviet people and tourists, background of ships, Murmansk harbor

tourist some quick but accurate insight. Some tourists fly in and out of a village in a day, which may seem frustratingly short, but often there are no overnight accommodations.

It seems that everybody is going north one way or another, except in the Soviet arctic where few tourists are admitted. In the rest of the north, villages that were virtually unheard of a few years ago have become famous as air terminals, such as Resolute and Inuvik in Canada; Kotzebue and Deadhorse in Alaska; and Sondre Stromfjord and Narssarssuaq in Greenland. Executives from Texas, tourists from Japan, oil tycoons from Iran, and hikers, scientists, miners, pipeline workers, and government officials from all over mingle in a mad confusion of boots and baggage when the big jets come into the new arctic airports where the toilets may or may not flush, and the food, if any, will cost a packet.

Around the fringe will inevitably be a group of local young people in jeans and western jackets, smoking, sipping soft drinks from the vending machines, chewing gum, and thinking who knows what about these strange newcomers.

The one necessary item to have for arctic touring is money, plenty of it, for travel costs a royal ransom on the crown of the world.

9
Arctic Animals:
A Renewable Resource

++

When we planned the trip looking at our map of the crown of the world we imagined many more animals than we actually saw. In fact, we were fearful of polar bears when we first began our arctic tenting. And with good reason, for we know that people are killed by bears every year.

What we did discover on the trip was a new attitude toward animals, a new relationship between men and animals that we miss in Western society generally. Man depends on animals in the arctic, and because he depends on them he loves, cherishes, and respects them, even though he kills them.

We never encountered a polar bear except for seeing skins being dried outside a lucky hunter's house. We did see whales, seals, walrus, and musk-oxen. Fish, birds, and tiny creatures of land, air, and sea we met in abundance, and we learned, when slapping a mosquito, that even that pest has a function in the chain of arctic life.

The arctic animals gave us sobering thoughts that are still not totally resolved in our minds. One thing is certain: pet animals on leashes are not part of the arctic scene.

++

WHY DID ancient man come to the hostile arctic in the first place? He was following the animals, for food and fur. In the nineteenth century, explorers in the North American arctic saw piles of mammoth and mastodon bones, a record of ancient ani-

Sheep and flowers in deep grass on Grimsey Island. This spot is probably directly on the Arctic Circle.

mal migration. These animals became extinct, probably due to changing climate and overhunting. Later, fur traders and whalers came, nearly wiping out other species of sea and land animals.

There are still numerous animals in the arctic such as polar bears, seals, whales, and walrus, in the water or on the ice. There are reindeer and their cousins the caribou, wolves, moose, and others in the tundra and taiga. Dozens of smaller creatures abound on land and sea, twice as many in the sea as on land. The air is seasonally full of birds that come each year, a whole heaven full, and then go away when it gets too cold. And in the tundra and taiga there are mosquitoes by droves and clouds, more than most people think are necessary.

As an offhand opinion one might think the polar bear is the most important animal on the land and that the whale is the most vital creature in the sea, ruling their special kingdoms in an independent fashion. But there are small creatures that are even more important: the land's mouselike rodent, the lemming, and the tiny sea organisms in the plankton, which is a floating mass of marine life. These insignificant-seeming living things control the life of the arctic because they are the beginnings of chains of life where one creature is dependent upon another for food. There is no superfluous life in the arctic, and in nature there is no waste.

In the spring when the sun comes and leads, or openings, form in the ice, minuscule single-celled plants, called phytoplankton, begin to grow like mad, millions upon millions of them in the open water or blooming under thin ice, using the sun for energy

Old print shows Eskimo hunting seals.

and the nutrients in the water for growth. Sea nutrients come from an undersea compost supply composed of dead organic matter, animal feces, and other wastes. The phytoplankton moves at the mercy of currents, and like all plants releases oxygen and uses carbon dioxide, for the benefit of creatures which must breathe oxygen. Within these floating plants live microscopic sea animals called zooplankton, which feed on the plants and multiply. The zooplankton and phytoplankton together form plankton, a rich, floating dinner table for sea creatures, from sea birds to whales. Baleen, the pliable substance inside the mouth of some types of whales, is meant to strain the plankton from sea water for a digestible whale meal.

Plankton, which is sometimes several meters thick, is a noisy scene. Sea birds hover over it, diving for the little fish that have

Terns fill the sky at Grimsey Island in Iceland's Arctic region.

attached themselves to it for the free ride. There is underwater sound from it too, attracting the free-swimming sea creatures in the water. When fishermen see the birds hovering over a mass of plankton they head for it, knowing that fish and sea mammals will be following for food. The remnants, crumbs from the table, so to speak, sink to the bottom for the sponges, crustaceans, clams, and bottom fish. Without plankton, there would be no sea life in the arctic.

If the plankton is the hero of the sea, then the lemming is the hero of the tundra. The lemmings' story might begin with the raven flopping overhead watching for a telltale sign of lemming tracks on the snow. In winter's darkness the lemming have lived under the snow, surviving on lichens and heat-holding roots, and in the process doing terrible damage to plant life. They give birth to their first litter in March, and in a good lemming year there may be births every month, bringing thousands upon thousands of new lemmings bouncing out onto the snow or ground where the ravens, snowy owls, gulls, foxes, and occasionally even caribou grab them for food. In the high birth years, which seem to run in four-year cycles, the foxes, breeding in lemming season, produce healthier cubs and larger litters. When the fox population rises, their feces fertilize more ground, making more lichen and plant life. Any animal den can be spotted on the tundra for there is green growth in the fertilized soil.

In the natural state, when animals are more plentiful, man survives and thrives. Dogs, on whom man was once dependent for transportation to the hunting grounds, eat the feces of man. Some explorers of the past tell of how no human could defecate in safety without a helper to beat off the dogs, which are kept hungry so they will operate the sled efficiently. People and animals have a close relationship in the arctic. There is kinship with, and reverence for, all creatures, but there are no orgies of sentimental attachments as seen in the pet syndrome of western civilization.

Even the bothersome mosquito has a function. The arctic char, a fish that provides delicious food both fresh and dried, feed on mosquito larvae. Mosquitoes annoy humans and animals alike. (It is only the female that bites, however, and the females do not

Dogs were once the primary means of transportation in the Arctic.

swarm. The deadly female works alone!) The mosquitoes' swarming drives the caribou and reindeer to the cooler areas. If these browsing animals did not migrate to escape the insects, the tundra where they winter would turn into a desert from excessive use.

Pesticides to control mosquitoes have nearly wiped out the peregrine falcon, which is now being painstakingly restocked at the University of Alaska. If birds, which naturally control insects, are killed with the pesticides, then the natural chain of life goes out of control. Even if bird-safe pesticides were used for mosquito control, what would the birds eat?

If the world should glaciate and snowfields became ice caps, as they did in the beginning of the Pleistocene age, and the fifteen million square miles of polar ice increased radically, turning away the sun's heat, land animals that could not adapt to cold would become extinct. *Arctic animals of land and sea are a renewable resource, which oil is not.* This is the point of arctic animal conservation, and any exploitation that leads to breaking the chain of life, the feeding patterns, and the movement of herds is cosmically shortsighted.

Overfishing by large ships has led to the extension of fishery limits by most countries of the world. The practices of one nation affect another even in remote international waters when bottom-scooping operations remove sea creatures heading for natural spawning spots. An example is the Alaska salmon whose future is

Alyeska pipeline crossing Alaska

insecure from Pacific Ocean fishing practices.

Pipelines and people affect caribou migrations. If the lemmings' land is disturbed by population shifts north, their important function will be endangered. If an oil rig destroys the eider ducks' nesting grounds, we will have no eiderdown. Who is to say if oil or the eider is more important? The warm down that lines the eider nest has traditionally protected mankind, and it could do so again if factories for making artificial fibers were forced to cease operations.

If the chain of life is not interrupted and breeding stock and conditions are wisely preserved in the arctic, it could mean the survival of man. Ancient arctic man proved that vegetables are not necessary to sustain life. He got them secondhand from the internal organs of sea mammals which fed on the plankton, or from the partially digested browse in the stomach of a freshly killed caribou.

Conservationists have been concerned with game management in the north for more than a century, with both good and bad results. The Russian fur traders of the eighteenth century virtually wiped out the sea otter in Alaska, but now the otter has been restored almost too well, according to fishermen whose livelihood is disturbed by too many protected sea otters. On the other hand, the musk-ox, almost extinct a few decades ago, is now thriving in Greenland, the Canadian islands, Spitsbergen, and Alaska. Experiments in using the musk-ox, whose odd behavior of forming a circle to protect its young against predatory animals made it a perfect target for man with a rifle, were tried in Vermont, but the results were not satisfactory. The musk-ox has no sweat glands, making its life nearly impossible out of the arctic. However, the University of Alaska is running a successful experimental musk-ox farm.

One animal experiment, done with the best intentions a century ago, interfered with nature to bring some long-term unexpected results. Missionary Sheldon Jackson and Captain M. A. Healy of the United States Revenue Service were impressed by both the

Old print of animals of Canada includes musk-ox.

Polar-bear skin drying on a classic umiak secured to whalebone supports, Point Hope, Alaska

prosperity of the Siberian Native people, who had ample reindeer for food, fur, and transportation, and the starvation of the Alaskan Eskimos across the Bering Strait. In the 1880's they arranged for the United States government to buy reindeer, which closely resembled Alaska's native caribou, as the latter were decreasing in number. Congress agreed to pay for an Eskimo reindeer-cultivation project, and about twelve hundred of the animals were imported from Siberia with Lapp herders to assist.

When gold-rush miners came into Alaska, the reindeer meat fed the influx of people. In 1914 Alaska had sixty-five herds, two-thirds of which were owned by Eskimos. The reindeer multiplied until there was nothing left of the lichen browse for the wild caribou to eat. Canada meantime purchased part of the United States herd and established it in the Mackenzie Delta. By 1932, over 600,000 reindeer were roaming over arctic Alaska. Out of control, they began to decrease drastically due to overpopulation; they had been allowed to increase beyond the ability of the land to support them. The tundra is fragile and it takes many decades for the lichens to grow back.

Reindeer all but disappeared in Alaska, but now with better knowledge of game management the NANA corporation is using

Polar-bear skin drying at Resolute on Cornwallis Island. Note perma-frost construction beneath prefabricated house.

some of its Native Claims Settlement money to reestablish reindeer herds for profit. In the late 1970's there have been cooperative meetings between Soviet native reindeer collective operators and Alaskan Eskimos.

The Soviets have pioneered in building a fish-hatching farm on the permafrost in an area where the temperatures go to $-72°$ F ($-58°$ C). When hydroelectric stations on the northern rivers interfered with fish production, Soviet fish experts were called in to help restore the losses. According to Soviet sources, the experiment in far northern fish hatching that used 100 million eggs, or roe, of several varieties of fish was so successful that now the fish are being distributed throughout the Soviet north. This should have a far-reaching effect on the northern fishing industry if the experiment continues to succeed.

Lemming experiments are being conducted at Tromsö, Norway, in the heart of Lapland, where the world's northernmost major university sponsors a biological experimental farm with special emphasis on arctic problems.

Conservation laws are in effect in every arctic country, but the governments have differing needs and attitudes. In Canada, for example, the federal government allows a polar-bear quota for

Canadian Inuit with walrus tusks

each Native settlement, and the persons within that area must decide who will be issued the permits. This makes it possible for the best hunters to ensure meat for all, in the customary Inuit sharing.

In spite of a number of international treaties there are no general arctic animal conservation laws. Seal hunting is economically important to the Canadian Native people, but the United States, with a different set of laws and pressures, will no longer allow seal skin and walrus ivory items to be imported. The effect has been a heavy economic blow to Canadian Native carvers and hunters who have lost one of their prime markets; yet they continue to kill the animals for food and clothing.

The most publicized and passionate issue before the public now is the save-the-whales movement. The International Whaling Commission is composed of fifteen member countries that are working to restore one of nature's most marvelous machines. In a miraculous process, whales can transform the free and ever growing plankton into edible protein for humans and useful oil for machines, a totally renewable resource factory that could be utilized by intelligent people. But the history of whaling is a sorry story of greed and thoughtless destruction.

When the International Whaling Commission met in Tokyo in December, 1977, to attempt to set further controls on commercial whaling, Alaskan and Canadian Native people begged to be heard. Ceremonial village whaling has long been a part of life where the whale was a vital source of food. Representatives from the North Slope Borough in Alaska asked that they not be held to the IWC quotas, speaking emotionally of how their whaling pattern was not in any way comparable with the methods of massive factory ships that can do irreparable harm. There was truth in their stand: in some small villages experienced elders lead a whaling expedition in the old formal manner following their cultural pattern of reverence for nature's bounty and total use of the whale. On the other hand, some places in Alaska and Canada have rotting whales lying on beaches, where irresponsible Natives have left them. Some enraged citizens, both Native and White, insist on the need for legal controls when such miraculous creatures are violated.

Rotting whale meat in the sand on the Chuckchi Sea

Bringing in the whale meat at Point Hope, Alaska

Slicing the muktuk from the whale

Whale meat being cooked in tent for whalers watching on the ice. The wives of whalers prepare traditional foods for the men.

Biologists know that there is much to be learned from the bodies of animals. No machine has yet produced fabric to equal the caribou skin which makes the warmest parka of them all. The hair is hollow so a caribou-skin tent is fine for getting across a stream since it can float. The traveling Eskimo family can bundle up its gear inside the tent to cross the stream. Musk-ox hair is now being woven into an expensive experimental fabric that is light, warm, and waterproof. Bird feathers, used for clothing in the past in the arctic, provide a layering principle that man could copy to keep his body warm in a cold house. Sled dogs, sleeping outside in bitter weather, instinctively curl up and breathe through their bushy tails. Physicians have borrowed this idea and recommend that a person breathe through a wool scarf, a fur ruff, or a special nose cone to prevent the shock of too much cold air entering the lungs, a situation that could trigger a heart attack. Man is the only creature that heats his house. The rest heat themselves, not their surroundings.

How do the arctic mammals survive in the polar water? A man will die of hypothermia, the too rapid loss of body temperature, within a few minutes after being immersed in the Arctic Ocean. Some biologists believe the arctic mammals have a natural antifreeze in their systems. If this could be isolated to use for man, then a possible new ice age might be more bearable.

The polar Eskimos who survived under the most bitterly cold conditions on earth did it with the aid and example of animals, their brothers and a continually renewable resource.

One creature found throughout the north is the raven, who stays in the arctic the year round. This awkward, flopping bird provides the people with endless amusing folk stories. In fact, Raven is considered the source of life in much ancient mythology. He is not good for eating or pulling sleds or providing warm clothes, but he gives advice. Anyone who has been in an arctic village has heard the croaking raven, squawking out his comments on the situation in his almost human voice. He interrupts, corrects, curses, and jeers at the human scene, making his political and social remarks available to those who can understand his language.

Small footnote: Ravens have recently begun nesting in New England, in an area unprecedented for such in local human memory. Are the ravens warning us of a new ice age, in which they will be able to live in arctic comfort farther south? Listen.

10

People and Politics

++

It seemed obvious from looking at the mass of arctic ice on our polar map that the people who had lived there must have been forced north by groups from below. When we reached the arctic and began to know its people we realized that the early inhabitants had learned to adjust to the environment. Only the hardiest lived, leaving a tough group of survivors.

Now the rugged minority group throughout the inner arctic is in conflict with people and governments over the mineral resources that have been found on the vast bleak traditional hunting lands of the Native people. We saw this pattern throughout the arctic, whether we were tenting in a Native village in Canada, resting up in a resort hotel in Lapland, or reading some of the many local books and newspapers giving minority points of view.

Native people are concerned about their future. We talked about it, when the language barrier permitted, over seal-meat stew on the ice, tea in a warm house, or beer in a friendly bar.

++

ABOUT A million people live within the Arctic Circle, a motley of ethnic and political bodies. There are Norse Icelanders on Grimsey Island; Eskimos, Indians, and Whites in Alaska; Eskimos, Indians, Whites, and Metis (ma-tey—persons of mixed White and Indian ancestry who have established themselves as a political group) in Canada; Lapps, Norwegians, Finns, and Swedes in Scandinavia; Greenlanders who are a hardy people of Eskimo and Danish stock, a few polar Eskimos, and Danes in

OPPOSITE PAGE: *Carver
at work.*

RIGHT: *Inuit writes to the
seal he hopes to shoot.*

BELOW: *This message to
the seal, written in syllabics on a piece of drift-
wood by a patient hunter
waiting for good luck,
uses a comic-book style.*

Greenland; the Chuckchis, Yakuts, Yukagirs, Eskimos, Lapps, Dolgans and other smaller native groups, and European Russians in the Soviet Union.

The Native people within the Circle had certain striking similarities before White Europeans encroached from the south. From North America to Europe to Asia, the Native people historically were nomads whose precarious lives depended on hunting on sea or land, whether they lived on the barren seacoast, river banks, tundra, taiga, or beside mountains and fiords. They cooperated in the hunt, regarding their animal prey as their brothers.

There had to be ceremonial propitiation, an apology to the soul of the "brother" for taking his life in the hunt. The rituals varied, but the spirit of reverence for nature was there. The people returned salmon skeletons to the rivers and gave a seal bone back to the ocean, and had elaborate formalities surrounding the killing of a bear. Figures of animals were endlessly and lovingly carved in ivory or bone or wood, and the weapons of death—spears, harpoons, and arrows—were decorated to beautify the killing of the animal.

Inuit woman prepares sealskin for making kamiks, *warm shoes.*

Ulu, *traditional knife used for scraping hair from seal in preparation of skin for making clothing*

Northern women worked together with summer berry picking, fish drying, and the making of skin garments. There was joint ownership of traditional hunting land and its resources, because the only means of survival was by a communal life. There was protocol in the division of meat, and everyone had a share. Scarcity precluded waste. Every part of the animal was eaten, except polar-bear liver which contains so much vitamin A that it is poisonous to humans! Stomachs filled with partially digested vegetation were highly prized for salads.

One of the celebrated Eskimo customs was to settle quarrels by lampooning, or dueling with ridicule, joking, singing and drumming until one of the embattled pair cracked under the taunts. Of course, there were deviations from this happy set of generalities, such as nasty tribal warfare and a prevailing enmity between Eskimos and Indians, and some cruel fights among the ancient Siberian people. But barring the human condition of petty greed, dealt with by local systems of tribal justice, the Native people shared their goods and every man was his brother's keeper.

They also shared poverty, illiteracy, starvation, and disease. They handled these problems the best they could, sometimes by infanticide or voluntary geriatricide when there was not enough food to sustain the group. There was cannibalism in extreme cases.

For medical and spiritual help they had a shaman, or witch doctor. This special man, woman, or, in rare cases, a child—with drums, dreams, incantations, trances, fetishes, familiars, and occult powers—was supposed to bring good luck to the hunt, heal the sick, and make contact with the spirits of the earth and sky and waters. Shamans had enormous power, power that sometimes became so corruptive that they became sources of evil in some cases.

And then White men began to infiltrate the arctic, bringing a whole new set of problems that were remarkably similar in each of the arctic cultures. The Native people and their lands were all exploited by the European Whites when the latter began expanding into the arctic before the seventeenth century. The finger points at Americans, Canadians, Norwegians, Swedes, Finns,

Inuit woman

Eskimo woman, wife of whaling boat captain, prepares to fry doughnut for incoming whalers.

This Indian woman will smoke her share of caribou meat with willow in Canadian arctic Yukon.

Danes, and Russians and their Soviet successors. Native people have been neglected, overlooked politically, and treated like children by their governments. Today Natives throughout the arctic are protesting what they consider lack of respect. It is hard to know what the Natives in the Soviet Union think, for their problems are not revealed to the rest of the world.

Native ways of life have been studied by social scientists, sometimes as if the Natives were a subhuman species. A horrible extreme was an otherwise respected early anthropologist who went into spasms of joy at finding intact a whole Eskimo village where the inhabitants had starved to death. It gave him such a splendid opportunity to study the bodies and houses without being disturbed.

The Natives were at the mercy of the guilt and benevolence of western civilization when a mixed bag of missionaries began to infiltrate on the heels of explorers, merchants, and profiteers. White man's alcohol made a big hit in the north from the first drink offered to a Native, and missionaries tried to combat this destructive evil which became a curse in the north. There are several theories about the intense attraction and effect of alcohol among the northern Natives. Is it an inborn heritage, a yearning to be turned into an instant powerful shaman who escapes the world in self-induced trances? Or is it the residual trace of mongoloid genes that are hostile to alcohol, for it appears that Asian people have low tolerance for hard liquor. The seeds of political problems of language, education, medicine, and religion were planted as Native people came to depend on western trade goods and the missionary education and medicine.

The first of the Native people to feel the impact of White European culture were the Samers or Lapps, a classic prototype for the history of Native-White contact. Traditionally the Lapp-marks, or Samer country, extended nearly a thousand miles, running along the Arctic Ocean from the present day Soviet Union through Finland, Sweden, and Norway. Today there are an estimated 36,000 Lapps, most of whom live in arctic Norway. Roughly a thousand years ago the Lapps began to have considerable contact with Norse Vikings who raided and traded with the Native people who roamed across the constantly changing national borders. The Lapps hunted reindeer and fished and spoke a common Finno-Ugraic language (which now has nine dialects). By the sixteenth century a few Norse and Russian people from the south decided to settle and farm in the frontier area, to the extent that Sweden passed a law forbidding this, declaring that all the Lappmarks belonged to her. Norway, Finland, Russia, and Denmark objected, and war broke out.

Sweden lost her arctic seacoast, but many Lapps were left in the interior. The Swedish kings had been promoting reindeer breeding and had already sent missionaries to the region. Whatever the royal motives were, and they were probably the best, the missionaries changed the Lapp life-style, for with the churches

142

Old print shows life on the tundra.

came schools and new customs, including taxes, which were paid
in furs.

The same pattern developed in all the Scandinavian countries
and in Russia. In the latter part of the seventeenth century the
discovery of silver in Lapland brought more changes. Reindeer
were used to transport the ore, and Lapps were, sometimes forci-
bly, put to work as laborers. Meanwhile zealous Lutheran missionaries tried to drive out the shamans. One Native, Anders
Nilsson, attacked a Lutheran priest who had taken away his
magic drum. Nilsson was punished by being burned alive by the
authorities.

Russians sent Orthodox priests to the Lapps in the Kola
Peninsula area and exacted furs from the people, tried to eradi-
cate shamanism, and so on. (Cossacks were collecting fur tributes
for the Czar from arctic Siberian Natives as well.) In defense of
the missionaries, the Lapps today concede that there were ex-
tremely good men among them. One was Per Fjellstrom, who
provided the Lapps with a written language. He translated the
New Testament into Lappish as well as writing down much of the
ancient Samer lore. In 1751, the Scandinavian countries arrived at
a remarkably humane treaty, for that day, which allowed the
Lapps to move freely over political borders, and a line was drawn

143

Lapp couple board bus for holiday.

to prevent further northern settlement.

But later when conscientious governments tried to provide general education for the Lapps, instruction for the most part was in Finnish, Norwegian, or Swedish, not in the Lappish dialects, a cultural catastrophe that is being remedied today. In Norway, for example, there is now a Lapp roving superintendent who sees to the language welfare of students in public schools. But the children of reindeer herders were, up until quite recent times, sent to regional boarding schools, separating children from their own people and native tongue.

Lapps were increasingly absorbed into the majority populations of Scandinavia, but after World War II when the entire world began to see a new rise in ethnic interest, cultural preservation societies, usually sparked by the growing number of highly educated Lapps and liberal academics, finally were merged into the Nordic Lapp Council in 1953. One of the tasks of the minority organization was to define a Lapp. The popular notion of Lappish culture is associated with reindeer herding, but by the 1950's

Lapland was filling up with snow machines, and herders were settling in towns. So language came to be the point of definition, and it was agreed that a Lapp is a person who (or whose parents or grandparents) learned Lappish as the first spoken language.

Good roads have brought increasing tourism to Lapland, actually intensifying the ethnic movement. There is an us-against-them attitude as camera-snapping tourists from the south spill from their cars to buy reindeer horns and other Lapp souvenirs, which the Lapps are not reluctant about selling. Some of the more radical Lapps want their ancestral lands returned. There is a renewed interest in learning the old language and in the traditional *yoik*ing, a unique kind of Lapp singing. The colorful Lapp costume is worn with pride.

Alf Esak Keskitalo, an official of the Sami Institute in the Norwegian Lapp capital of Kautokeino, sat at his desk in an ordinary business suit in 1977, but he said that if he went traveling or to an official meeting or formal social occasion he would wear his native dress. Reindeer herders usually wear the traditional ancient costume.

One of the most vocal and best known of the Lapps today is Israel Ruong, professor of Lappish Language and Ethnology at the University of Uppsala, Sweden. Another internationally known Lapp is Nils-Aslak Valkeapaa, poet, musician, and

Lapp souvenir stand at Ivalo, Finland

Eskimo child, Point Hope, Alaska

teacher, who carries his Lapp culture and his shaman's drum to people throughout the north.

The Alaskan Eskimos, who number 24,000 today, were the next Native group to have massive White contacts. When the Russians began moving east across Siberia to the Pacific in search of furs, they finally, at the end of the eighteenth century, established a Russian colony in southern Alaska, to the grief of the local Indians and Aleuts. The arctic Eskimos had little communication with these Russians, but by the nineteenth century Yankee and European whalers were off the Alaska coasts slaughtering whales for corset stays and oil. They were followed by traders bringing their classic gifts of new diseases, guns, alcohol, beads, calico, and seductions, in exchange for furs and favors. Missionaries, explorers, scientists, and finally tourists followed.

When Russia sold Alaska to the United States in 1867, the Treaty of Cession carried this clause: "The uncivilized tribes will be subject to such laws and regulations as the United States may, from time to time, adopt in regard to aboriginal tribes in that country." This linked the fate of Native people of the north to the American Indians. Of course, Russia had never bought the land from the Natives in the first place, so, it was to be argued later, how could they sell it to the United States?

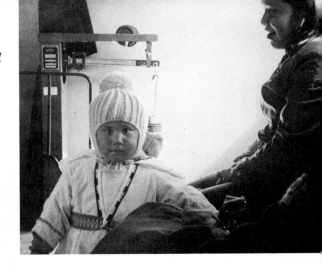

Inuit child

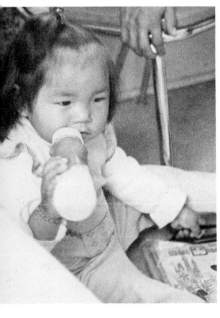

Inuit child

Eskimo children

When the Russians departed, the Natives of Alaska rocked along in neglect and poverty under United States military rule. In 1844, however, their status was improved when the so-called Organic Act made Alaska a federal district with an appointed governor, and protection for lands used by the Natives was promised. It was 1924 before all Natives were granted citizenship.

Meantime, the education, medical care, welfare and religion of the arctic Natives were in the hands of missionaries. Sheldon Jackson, a minister of intelligence and concern for the Natives (he was the person who persuaded the government to import the reindeer from Siberia), convinced the Congress to allot money for Native education. Congress obliged in 1890, coming across with the princely sum of $25,000 to run an educational system for an area twice the size of Texas.

In the face of the penurious government, missionaries picked up the challenge to build schools, write dictionaries, and furnish medical help, as well as run churches. Until quite recent times, English-speaking, church-run boarding schools were the major or only way for arctic Native children to get an education. But parents objected to the separation from their children, and the gradually widening generational gaps often caused a breakdown in the traditional language, religious, and subsistence patterns.

The greatest single event to bring White men to the arctic in Alaska and elsewhere in the north was World War II. Every

Eskimo child is overwhelmed by village utility truck in Alaska.

arctic country was forced to take tax money from the total populations to improve transportation to the north in the military emergency. Until this threat forced southern governments to take a look at their arctic people, hardly any public tax money was spent on the arctic.

In Alaska many air fields and the new Alcan (later called the Alaska) Highway brought servicemen in staggering numbers. The United States arctic Eskimos joined up as volunteers in the vital Alaska Territorial Guard. There was no going back to the old days. In the cold war of the 1950's, White impact continued to grow when the series of early warning stations, such as the Dew Line, were built across the arctic. The men who came to operate these stations had considerable contact with the Native people, who noted with interest the new machines, movies, and heavy equipment used at the sites.

In 1959 Alaska became the forty-ninth American state. In the Statehood Act, Alaska was given the right to choose 103 million acres of Federal land. Nothing was said about Native land rights except that Congress agreed not to interfere with previous land rights or titles of the Natives. Yet the Federal government already owned most of Alaska so what was left for the Natives, other than discontent and suspicion?

In the 1960's things happened in a hurry. The Eskimos, increasingly aware of their rights as citizens, were alarmed when the Federal government made plans to set off a nuclear explosion to create an artificial harbor at Fort Thompson on the Chuckchi Sea for the shipment of minerals from northwest Alaska. In 1961, the Eskimos organized to fight Project Chariot, as it was called. They stopped the blast, and the new spirit of unity kept rolling. By 1962, the *Tundra Times*, a new Eskimo newspaper edited by the late Howard Rock, became the mouthpiece for the aroused arctic Native people who were incensed by the poor housing, poverty, discrimination, the rising number of people forced to depend on welfare, and a snake pit of social problems—from controversial federal controls over traditional hunting to the need for more local schools.

A new radical left, especially among the young people, was

149

A whaling captain at the ready beside his Umiak on the Chuckchi Sea

spearheaded by Charles "Etok" Edwardsen, Jr., of Barrow. Etok contended that Alaska belonged to the Natives. In 1965 a group organized the Arctic Slope Native Association (ASNA) and filed claim to ownership of all their traditional land, 88,281 square miles. Such a wrangle arose that by 1966 Secretary of the Interior Stewart Udall imposed a land freeze on Alaska's federal lands so that no transfer could occur until the Native claims were settled. Since most of Alaska's land was under federal control, the state rocked in alarm.

In 1967 a bill to settle Native land claims was considered, but not passed, by Congress. It might have been there yet had not a new element entered the scene. Oil, massive quantities of it, was discovered at Prudhoe Bay on state land. Oil companies went wild to join the drill. When the state of Alaska held a sale of oil and gas leases in September, 1969, Etok and his young followers picketed the affair, bringing their cause to worldwide attention on television.

The state of Alaska made $900 million on the lease sale, but the oil companies were in trouble. They could not build the pipeline to get the oil from Prudhoe to the port at Valdez as long as the political land freeze was in effect, for the pipeline would have to pass over federal lands. These lands would not be released until the Native claims were settled.

So the world's most unlikely pair of political bedfellows were joined—the oil companies who were out to make money and a radical group of young Eskimos who claimed that all of Alaska was theirs anyhow. Oil executives, seeing that no oil would flow until the Native claims were settled, went to work to get the government moving. Ordinarily oil companies would not care in the least about land claims of a remote minority group, but with the corporations' self-interest at stake a massive lobby for Native land claims was begun.

The Alaska Native Claims Settlement Act (ANCSA) was passed on December 18, 1971. By its terms Alaska Native people won the most staggering settlement in history—forty million acres of land and $462.5 million with an additional $500 million in revenue from certain mineral resources.

All United States citizens who could prove one-quarter or more Alaska Eskimo, Indian, or Aleut blood alive at the time of the settlement would receive benefits. The distribution would be handled through twelve modern corporations throughout Alaska. The Natives as stockholders would get dividends through corporation investments.

There was much to be done—land selection, decisions on investment of money, and planning. Not everybody was happy over the settlement, for some of the Natives wanted the entire state. But nobody argued that this was an unprecedented piece of legislation for Native people. The Native corporations that lie within the Arctic Circle are the Arctic Slope Regional Corporation, the Northwest Alaska Native Association (NANA), and a small part of Doyon, Ltd. These corporations are busy today building hotels, performing services, improving their villages, and answering to stockholders in proper legal corporation style.

While American Alaskan Natives were fighting for and winning their land claims settlement, their 15,000 Canadian Inuit relatives

GAMES DAY
Ellesmere Island

Cooking seal meat

Tea-boiling contest

The winner!

Village games

Inuit faces, Canada

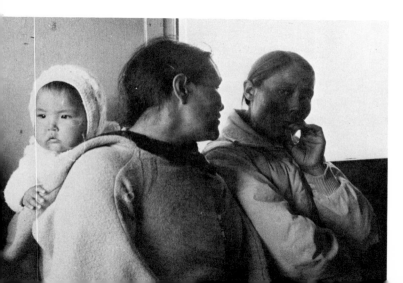

across the border were involved in land claims of their own. In the Canadian arctic, which lies in the Northwest Territories and the Yukon Territory, besides the Inuit there are the Denes (danay) or Athapaskan Indian people, and the Metis. Whatever the ethnic background of the people, their history of grievances was much the same as the other people of the north. The Hudson's Bay Company was the chief instrument of contact and change, followed in the nineteenth century by the famed Northwest Mounted Police, the civil police force which became known in time as the Royal Canadian Mounted Police or the RCMP. The RCMP has enforced Canadian federal law in the Territories for many years, with units in most villages. Nowadays a uniformed Native assistant, usually the best paid and most influential local person in the village, is part of most RCMP operations.

An especial Canadian affliction has been the multiplicity of languages. Separated physically by islands, peninsulas, and rugged terrain as well as the ethnic backgrounds, Canadian Natives have never operated as a single force. When the spoken language differences—Inuit regional dialects, English and French patois, half a dozen Indian tongues—are added, the separation becomes wider. The final calamity seemed to come about 1875 when a well-intentioned Anglican missionary, the Reverend Mr. Edmund Peck, with a genius for linguistics, tried to give his Inuit charges a written language so they could read the Bible and the Book of Common Prayer.

The story of *syllabics*, the unique written language of the Canadian Inuit, began in 1823 when an inventive young Methodist missionary, the Reverend Mr. James Evans, who had been a Baltic Sea sailor, was sent to preach the Gospel to the Ojibway Indians in Canada. Mr. Evans was instructed to translate the Bible into the Ojibway dialect, which tongue he had quickly mastered, and transcribe it in the Roman alphabet. But James Evans had also been a clerk and was interested in the efficiency of writing. The dialect he was working with had long descriptive terminology, so he set out to invent a sort of shorthand, a new orthography of nine symbols which could easily put the complex Indian tongue into a quickly learned written language. The mission board turned it down flat, and the invention went into a file. Twenty years later Evans tried his idea again in the Cree Indian dialect. This time he used hand-carved wooden type with soot and fish-oil ink to print his original orthography on birchbark. It was easy to learn, but it had little success among the Indians.

After Evans' death, the Reverend Mr. Peck, the Anglican missionary to the Inuit, was asked to adapt Evans' syllabic script for his church use, since it was suitable for the long words of *Inuktituk*, the Eskimo spoken language. By 1877 Peck had succeeded in teaching a few Inuit to read and write their own ancient language in the new letters. Mr. Peck became famous and beloved among the Inuit people, and his version of syllabics rapidly brought the magic of literacy to the Canadian arctic world. But the long-range effect has been to isolate a small group of people who only read and write in an obscure alphabet and who have little but church literature for written communication.

Despite the cold truth that Roman orthography is essential to reading today's press, some Inuit hold tenaciously to their now "traditional" form of writing. There are grave arguments within the Inuit community about the direction of their written language, and educators and government officials press for a change to the standard Roman alphabet.

As in the rest of the arctic, World War II opened the land and the minds of the people. A benign (or self-seeking, according to one's point of view) government in Ottawa knew something had to be done to relieve the economic situation of the arctic Natives who were complaining, with justification, about the Hudson's Bay Company monopoly, poor housing, lack of communication, and the dependence on welfare, as well as other distresses. Canada came up with a village Cooperative movement that has become a thriving success in many areas. Since the first locally run Co-Op was established in 1959, Co-Ops have become the largest employer of Inuit people in Canada. They run hotels, grocery stores, canneries, municipal services, and tourist enterprises, and organize marketing of carvings and other arts and crafts. In Aklavik and Tuktoyuktak, Co-Ops run entirely by women trap muskrat and wolf, process the skins, and sew high-quality fur parkas

Modern school, Old Crow, Yukon

which are marketed throughout Canada.

Until the 1960's most Canadian arctic education was in the hands of church boarding schools. Today a typical arctic village has a well-equipped, government-run school with certified teachers from the south. Nearly a hundred percent of children are in school as well as a fair number of adult students. There are Native aides whose function is often to teach the local tongue and to promote old crafts and customs. There are more Native certified teachers today. There is intense local interest in the schools which often serve as posh community centers as well. Carpeting,

Modern school at Grise Fiord, Ellesmere Island

good libraries, and a staggering array of electronic visual aids are increasingly the normal situation, not the exception.

The village may have a community hall as well, along with the RCMP post, a church, a Co-Op store with cake mixes and soda pop, a power-generating plant for lighting houses, a water delivery service, and sewage and garbage pickup. In Canada as well as in Alaska, communications systems with radio or satellite service put the remote areas in touch with the outer world, a service essential to the nursing stations which often need to contact doctors at central hospitals. Nurses in remote arctic areas are prepared by special training to handle more emergencies than the ordinary nurses in city hospitals.

There are a few dog teams, many snow machines, animal skins, horns, carcasses, drying fish, and meat scattered around the yards of the prefabricated houses. In the larger towns there might even be a hotel (expensive!) where the service does not match the price.

When Canadian and United States business began extensive explorations at the mouth of the Mackenzie River and in the Beaufort Sea, pipelines were already being planned. Natives whose lands were involved, and who were not consulted, saw the advantage of working together. The Committee for Original People's Entitlement (COPE) and the Indian Brotherhood of the Northwest Territories were established in 1970, soon followed by the Metis Association, the Council for Yukon Indians, and several other groups formed for mutual Native protection.

The Inuit Tapirisat of Canada (Eskimo Brotherhood), established in 1971, actually proposed in 1976 the creation of a new political state to be called Nunavut. Although this demand was formally withdrawn, the idea is not dead. Some governmental leaders, environmental groups, and the Canadian churches joined forces with the Native groups to stop development, especially the construction of pipelines, until the Natives' wishes were heard and land claims were settled.

The unrest of the 1970's led the Canadian government to set up hearings in 1975 so that people could voice their feelings. Justice Thomas Berger of the British Columbia Supreme Court con-

Indian children, the Yukon

ducted the Mackenzie Valley Pipeline Inquiry, holding meetings in thirty-five communities to hear from oil companies, town officials, environmental experts, and, most of all, the Native voices speaking in their own dialects to support or protest northern development.

When the Berger hearings finally ended in November, 1976, for the Natives at the crossroads the question seemed to boil down to "Do I want to be a second-class minority citizen in a wide world, or go back to the ways of my ancestors?" There seems to be no clear-cut answer as the conflict between Canada's oil development and Native claims remains unsettled.

When Eric the Red and his Icelandic friends set up the first known White colony in North America in southern Greenland in the year 982, they built their settlement on an ancient Sarqaq Eskimo site. A marker today says the Eskimos lived there from about four thousand to two thousand years ago.

The Norse people, who had the first republic in North America, disappeared from Greenland at about the end of the fourteenth century. Communication from Europe had ceased, and probably the colony was absorbed by the Sarqaq, Dorset, or Thule Greenlandic Eskimo cultures.

To cover the involved history of the world's largest island in a few sentences it should be noted that Greenland and its sturdy Natives were "claimed" first by Norway and then, by international political changes, fell into the hands of Denmark in 1814. Greenland, two-thirds of which is above the Arctic Circle, has been under Danish control and influence since that time. The Danish Royal Greenland Trading Company was given exclusive trading rights in Greenland and even today markets most of Greenland's arctic output.

Following the usual pattern in the far north, missionaries came on the heels of the merchants. The greatest and best known of them was Norwegian Hans Egede who felt a call to search for the long-lost Viking colony settled by Eric the Red in southern Greenland. He did not find out what had happened to the old

Old print of Norwegian on skis   *Statue of Leif Ericsson*

Viking settlers, but he did spread the Lutheran religion to the Native people.

When Egede reached Greenland, he found the Natives already racially mixed with the Dutch, German, and other Europeans, especially the Danish, but they had not seen European missionaries. Yet the old Vikings who had built the first settlement had constructed the first Christian church in the new world, for the wife of pagan Eric the Red was a Christian convert. The foundations of her church, a Roman Catholic chapel, can be seen today at Brattahlid in southern Greenland.

Egede put the spoken Greenlandic Inuit tongue into writing and translated the Bible into an awkward form of half-Greenlandic, half-Danish language. Later a Moravian missionary, Samuel Kleinschmidt, who was born in Greenland of missionary parents and educated in Germany, devoted his enormous talents to a true Greenlandic written language. So successful was he that literate Greenlanders have been able to share ideas with a common written language in the Roman alphabet for over a century. Greenland had the first arctic magazine when, in 1861, H. J. Rink, a Danish official in Greenland, encouraged Greenlanders to write down their old stories for their own pleasure. There was news, too, of the outer world. His Native helper Arqaluk edited and illustrated the magazine for years, using woodblocks and paintings by a noted local artist, Aron of Kangeq.

The Greenlanders are a sturdy lot. Like all Eskimos, they are highly artistic people, and thanks to their long-time written language they have a rich literature as well as brisk publishing and printing.

After World War II Greenland became more open to the world, and more bright young Greenlanders were sent to Denmark for higher education. Yet today there is no university in Greenland, and only 20 percent of the population speaks Danish, the language of higher learning for the country. More and more Greenlanders want to control their own country, despite, or because of, modern schools, good health care, police protection, welfare, libraries, and paternal concern by Denmark.

In 1953 Greenland became a political unit of Denmark, with locally elected members of Parliament to represent them in Copenhagen. It is now a part of Denmark, as the state of Alaska is part of the United States. Thoughtful governmental policy in Greenland has worked at keeping Native traditions and livelihood alive. When the Thule Air Force Base was established in 1952, the local people were moved to Qanaq, where, with government aid, they were protected from the nearby White community and encouraged to live in their traditional manner to prevent the dissolution of their culture. In other ventures, to promote employment and revenue, the government has invested heavily in fishing boats and processing plants, but this has resulted in bringing Natives to live in cities in cement-block apartment houses where welfare, alcoholism, and juvenile delinquency are the usual consequences for people who have grown up in a hunting culture.

Probably the largest international airport in the arctic is at Sondre Stromfjord, a joint Danish-United States operation. Although there are no scheduled direct flights from there to the United States or Canada, Europeans, including the Danish Royal

Little arctic resources—children of the Soviet Chukotka

Family, come in droves, and Danish Greenlanders go as often to Denmark. In all of Greenland there are only 45,000 people, of whom 7,000 are Danes who mostly come to earn high wages and return to Denmark to spend them.

There is active discontent in arctic Greenland. When Greenland joined the European Common Market in 1970, many of the Natives were in violent opposition to the agreement. Problems of fishing limits, which some believe benefit Denmark but not Greenland, are a cause of misunderstanding. On the other hand, many Copenhagen taxpayers feel that the cost of maintaining Danish Greenland is greater than the benefits. But oil being drilled for at Holsteinborg promises potential riches for Denmark.

Arctic Soviet politics are not open for discussion in a free press, but according to Soviet sources and some European observers, the transition from the traditional cooperative Native hunting, fishing, and reindeer herding in the north to the Soviet communes has not been too drastic a change from the old days. Hunting communes, for example, are given a minimum production quota, but incentive bonuses are paid so hunters continue in their old practices to some degree. Full-time hunters may well make more money than a factory worker by manipulating the incentive scheme.

Primary schools are conducted in the local dialects, which are now written in the Cyrillic alphabet, after some earlier experiments of using the Roman alphabet. Health care, education, and housing are said to be good or at least adequate for the less than three thousand Eskimos (no available figures on other Native groups). Since everybody is employed, whether he likes it or not, there is no welfare.

Although Canadian, French, and even United States missions have exchanged visits with Soviets, whatever political unrest or euphoria the arctic Soviet Natives feel is not likely to be honestly revealed.

So the varied peoples and their special political problems seethe in their own tide pool at the crown of the world.

11
Environmental Problems in the Arctic

✦✦

We knew there were special environmental problems in the arctic, but we had to see them to believe them. When we bent our tent pegs trying to drive them into the frozen earth we got a clearer picture of what it was like to build a house or a road on permafrost.

The problem of arctic waste disposal is a nightmare. We looked at the piles of bursting black plastic bags, the acres of rusting discarded equipment, the half-frozen, half-soggy mess of household trash and shuddered in our parkas, imagining the crown of the world on Judgment Day, buried under a sky-high blanket of used disposable diapers, for arctic babies use them too.

✦✦

If you want to preserve something, you put it on ice. The permafrost that underlies most of the arctic earth and sea margins is an icebox so effective that engineers there, dealing with the rising population, tourists, and modern ideas of sanitation, have a whole new set of problems when they face waste disposal. Preservation then becomes a curse.

The most obvious difficulty in the frozen earth is the inability to dig sewers and septic tanks to flush away human offal. With

Water is a scarce commodity in the north.

the exception of Scandinavia where the soil is warmer, towns above the Circle seek solutions to plumbing in elemental ways. Indoor toilets are lined with heavy plastic bags which are deodorized with chemicals, sealed with a twisted wire, and placed outside for the town truck to take away, if the town has such a service, to an open burning dump. The deodorizing chemicals are essentially embalming fluids which preserve the fecal matter and are themselves an environmental hazard. The plastic bags do not deteriorate and their burning makes a noxious smoke.

In some places there are frigid outdoor privies, and in other localities each family goes out daily to empty slops on the ice or in the water. Distasteful as this may be, the environmental risks are less since the refuse is a natural organic material that eventually breaks down into nutrients.

Getting water to a house and getting sewage away is managed in some of the larger communities by above-ground pipelines called utilidors. Often these heavily insulated pipes carry water,

166

heat, and electricity to a house, and take away the sewage. The strange arrangements of pipes that characterize the lucky arctic towns that have modern plumbing are costly and account in some measure for the high hotel rates—for plumbing is one of the luxuries you pay for in the arctic's tourist hotels.

If you live as most people do in the far north you are likely to carry your water from a village deep well, or bring in blocks of sea ice which you keep constantly melting on your kitchen stove. Laundry is a problem, and if you bathe very often you make your skin less resistant to the cold, so that the temptation to use the family's water supply for idle soaking goes down with the temperature. Fresh water is scarce in the arctic, and travelers are warned that the water is sometimes contaminated. Hepatitis is a constant danger.

The disposition of ordinary trash is another problem. Since it cannot be buried in the frozen ground it is usually burned in an

Villagers fill tanks with water at the town pump and load them onto snow machine for the mile journey to the settlement.

Typical arctic waste disposal

open dump; the smoke generated by the constant efforts to burn old tires, useless stoves, dead dogs, and grocery-store packaging pollutes the air.

As industry leaps north there is the matter of industrial waste. The Alyeska pipeline was required to provide the most modern of waste disposal measures. Inspectors saw to it that the premises were kept immaculate, and that a modern waste disposal plant was built to take care of the garbage caused by workers and

LEFT: *More arctic waste.* RIGHT: *An old car in an arctic village is a fascinating plaything.*

machines. The Native corporation NANA, as a money-making venture, runs a model waste disposal plant at Prudhoe for the oil companies. Trash and sewage can be removed but it costs a great deal of money to construct the buildings and buy the sophisticated machinery used in big cities farther south.

The Environmental Protection Agency has experimented with Alaska Village Demonstration Projects to set up models for central community facilities for safe drinking water, bathing, and solid waste disposal at Emmonak and Wainwright. Some imaginative inventors have produced "humus toilets," or cook-off organic privies, and other sanitary units that require no water and

*Victorian artist's conception of
the inside of Eskimo home*

can be used in permafrost areas. But the general trend of the manufacturing world is to try to adapt the water closet to a hostile environment. White people continue to try to carry their culture north, in spite of the lesson from explorers who found that the way to survive in the arctic is to adapt to Native ways.

Long ago the Natives heated their tiny turf and rock houses with blubber or whale oil. Today most buildings are expensively heated with oil, gas, or electricity. A few imaginative people are

ABOVE: *Pipes in gravel beneath building equalize temperature and prevent damage from permafrost.*

LEFT: *Detail of utilidor at Thule, Greenland*

thinking of experimenting with power generation by using their own waste, making methane gas that would give heat and power and at the same time destroy the waste. One veteran White schoolteacher in Point Hope, Alaska, has drawn plans for such an experiment, but like many local arctic projects it lacks government backing to date.

The study of permafrost began in earnest in the 1940's in North America during the building of the Alcan (Alaska) Highway. The Soviets, who had built new cities in the far north to utilize their rivers that flowed into the Arctic Ocean, had already begun intensive permafrost studies in the 1930's. One half of the USSR and Canada lie on permafrost, which is considered to exist when the subsurface ground remains at 32° F (0° C) for a year or more. The active surface layer, of course, will usually thaw in summer, but permafrost remains, as the word implies, permanently frozen.

Some of the ways builders combat the permafrost look like science fiction to the layman. One is to run refrigeration lines under a building so that the supporting soil will never melt and cause the building to sink or tip on its side. A building on permafrost disturbs the heat pattern of the ground, making the earth under the structure warmer and more likely to melt. If the melt is uneven it can eventually destroy a building by tearing it apart.

A common procedure is to build on gravel pads with drainage pipes, but gravel is a scarce commodity in the arctic. Some of the Canadian islands that are rich in gravel export it for good profit. At Resolute on Cornwallis Island, fat-bellied Hercules planes take off around the clock in the summer to deliver literal pay dirt to building and drilling sites, as oil rigs are usually set on gravel pads. To eliminate some of the permafrost problems, buildings are usually put on deeply embedded reinforced concrete or heavy wood pilings with an open wind space under the floor to ensure a

RIGHT: *Typical permafrost construction*

BELOW: *Special concrete is prepared for permafrost construction.*

Log houses are built above the ground in the few arctic areas where wood exists.

Ranger emergency hut in Canadian arctic with special construction to prevent wind destruction

cold layer on the ground. Of course, this brings a new set of problems, for it makes the house more difficult to heat with arctic winds constantly stealing underneath. Worse yet, light wooden structures on pilings are like toys in the hurricane winds that sometimes arise, so the buildings must be tied down with heavy cables. Scores of unmoored houses were blown to matchstick wood bits in a storm at Pangnirtung on Baffin Island in the winter of 1976.

The sensitive tundra above the permafrost creates environmental issues these days. Off-road vehicles leave tracks that cannot be erased in a lifetime. Even boot tracks last for years. So even getting the supplies to a building site must be done with utmost care.

Oil spills on the permafrost are another serious matter. The oil just lies there; it cannot sink through the permafrost. This is a point that conservationists bring forward when more oil pipelines are proposed. The problem of the spillage from the Alyeska pipeline in Alaska has not been totally solved, although efforts to remove surface oil spills are required by law. A major pipeline blowout would be a disaster.

Oil spills anywhere are damaging, but under the arctic ice oil is hard to locate and recover. In the north where the cold conditions keep the oil in a viscous state, a major oil spill could cause permanent ecological changes. Offshore oil drilling in the arctic presents dangers that have not yet been solved, or even completely faced. Arctic sea mammals are especially vulnerable to the impact of gas and oil extraction. There is a limited amount of open water along the ice pack, and it is needed for the breathing and feeding of seals, walruses, whales and other sea creatures. If it becomes clogged and the surface is covered with oil many of them will die. Polar bears would have oil clogged in their fur which would probably result in death. Sea birds, which provide nutrients to the sea, are especially sensitive to oil pollution. Oil spills under the ice from a well blowout would affect the algae under the ice in the spring. If oil seeps into the plankton and thus into the food chain it could cause the sea life literally to die. Oil spills affect the melt rate of ice which in turn affects breeding of

USS Queenfish. *The People
of the arctic fear atomic
pollution.*

mammals and fish, as well as having an ultimate effect on the
world's climate.

Nuclear accidents in the north are feared by the Natives. It was
nuclear Project Chariot that unified the Alaska Native people.
Throughout the arctic Native people fear that the uncaring majority from the south will use the barren lands of the north for a
nuclear dumping ground. The nuclear danger in the arctic had
front page interest in 1978 when radioactive material was strewn
over a large area in Canada's Northwest Territories from the
crash of a nuclear-powered Soviet satellite. It appeared that when
the crash seemed inevitable, the remote northern area was delib-
erately chosen for the scene. In the 1960's a United States bomber
carrying nuclear bombs crash-landed in northern Greenland.

Does the world regard the arctic as an expendable wasteland?

An arctic problem related to the environment is health. Water-borne diseases are on the rise as more people move into the north, bringing new germs and creating more waste. There are special cold-weather health hazards such as snow blindness, frostbite, hypothermia, intestinal parasites from eating uncooked meat—you can get trichinosis from walrus, for example.

Poor nutrition is a recent cause for concern. People who eat plenty of the traditional local meat and seafood are not often the victims; it is the uninformed people who load up on junk foods, found in the new-style grocery stores, who are suffering. Cold weather calls for high-fat diets, and health workers push nutrition education campaigns to promote high calories from healthier sources than soda pop and candy.

Dental problems are a constant curse. Some of these are due, especially among the women, to the old practice of chewing skins to soften them for sewing, but more often they are from too much sugar and chewing gum. It is not unusual to see people in their early twenties wearing false teeth.

There is a high incidence of anemia among the people of the north. An hereditary blood disease, methemoglobinemia, occurs only among Eskimos and Athapaskans.

Tuberculosis was the scourge of the arctic when people lived in crowded igloos. (The word igloo, by the way, means house, not necessarily the popular concept of a snow house. Most igloos were made of earth, skin, driftwood, and whalebones. One de-serted whalebone-and-sod igloo at Point Hope, Alaska, has, along with the crawl-in winter door, old electric lighting.) TB is no longer the killer it once was, although the pneumonia rate is high. Scurvy, the dietary disease that killed many early explorers who failed to follow Native diets, is no longer a problem.

Alcoholism and smoking are rampant health issues among the Native people. Smoking is so prevalent that lung cancer among Alaskan Eskimos has doubled in the last fifteen years, and rates for most other cancers are higher than in the rest of the United States.

Free medical service is available to this Inuit mother and child.

Free medical service for Native people is now provided by all governments within the Arctic Circle, and air transportation is provided to hospitals when necessary. By using the Canadian-American Communications Technology Satellite which was launched in 1976 there is two-way visual as well as audio connection from remote nursing stations through certain ground stations to medical centers. A terminal and broadcast studio is at the National Library of Medicine at Bethesda, Maryland.

There are concerned people, both Native and outsiders, who feel that opening the north for unlimited tourism would be an environmental disaster. Just what kind of effect and how great the harm would be has pitted thoughtful people against each other. National parks in the arctic, and there are many in almost every arctic country, seem at first glance to be a good idea. Yet some Native people feel that parks take a disproportionate amount of land from their control for the advantages of tourists. Parks could cause, rather than reduce, environmental problems since the animals are disturbed. A new problem that has not been really assessed is the unnecessary killing of animals, especially polar bears, which are attracted by the people who come north to work. The garbage around an oil pad, for example, is a natural food source to animals. If a worker should awaken to find a bear outside his Quonset hut, he would probably shoot it in self-defense, of necessity, for polar bears are dangerous. But the attractive nuisance of the human presence has then caused one more death in the diminishing polar-bear population.

It is claimed that no nation has a sensible arctic plan and that there is no international arctic policy. This is true to a great degree, but in every arctic country today there are planners in the process of working out rules and policies that will keep a balance between conflicting interests. When planners set to work, first there must be an assessment of what is there—the climate, geography, people, animals, historic sites, cultural uses of the land, and so on. Are there endangered species of animals or plants? Is the local culture endangered? What limitations should be set on developers? Whose "rights" are right? What environmental damage could be reasonably assumed to occur if a new industry were introduced?

There are, as one thoughtful taxpayer wryly noted, more "studies" than solutions for the environmental problems of the arctic.

Inuit ranger and friends at Auyuittuq National Park on Canada's Baffin Island

12

The Future of the Arctic

++

When we waited for the United States Air Force jet that would fly us to New Jersey from Greenland, we realized that we were very near Canada's Ellesmere Island, where we had camped the summer before. It was so close, we remarked, that we knew that the Eskimos from Greenland and Ellesmere visited each other over the winter ice on their dog teams. It was tempting to stay and try it ourselves.

But we had to think of our own futures. How would our map look to us now? We knew it would be filled with memories of cold tents, enchanting flowers, heavy packs, troubled Native people, a rape of resources, and warmth of the hearts of our new arctic friends.

We knew we would never again take for granted the convenience of a hot bath or efficient waste disposal, or the comfort of the soft bed under that ceiling map that started the whole thing.

++

FUTURISTICS IS everybody's game since it involves a little fantasy, a little hope, a little foolishness, a bit of the betting spirit, and a few hard facts. A lot of people are thinking of the future of the arctic these days—petroleum engineers, Native rights activists, bird lovers, grant seekers, and military establishments, among others.

One prediction that holds promise is that there will be more cooperation between the Soviet north and the rest of the arctic than there has been in the past. The Northern Sea Route convoys,

LEFT: *What does the future hold for this Eskimo child whose grand-parents are proudly presenting him to the summer sun?* RIGHT: *Will Native mothers continue to carry their children in their ample traditional hoods?*

once such a well-guarded secret, are now available, under some circumstances, for use by other nations. Although the Soviets did not participate in the Inuit Circumpolar Conference, shortly afterward Native contacts were opened when a Soviet Eskimo/ Chuckchi from Siberia was allowed by his government to spend a month in Alaska. Yuri Sergeevich Rytkheu, vice president of the Soviet Writers Union, who has written extensively on Soviet Native people, visited local Eskimos as well as officials at the University of Alaska. The interchange of information about reindeer culture between the Soviets and other arctic nations is a promising continuing cooperative effort.

International whaling and sealing control will probably grow in intensity as the world becomes more aware of the diminishing

Traditional and modern transportation meet in Soviet arctic.

species. The International Whaling Commission provides emotional front page news, and the likelihood is that there will be stronger controls placed upon Native whaling despite a lobby to the contrary.

The population of the arctic is predicted to grow, and the summer seasonal population will rise sharply. The needs and demands of industrialists and oil tycoons from Edmonton, Houston, Copenhagen, and Oslo who crowd into crude remote airports result in better air facilities and accommodations. This in turn leads to more tourism, as air and sea transportation extend the limits of northern horizons. Especially promising in North America are short tours, one day (or one night) jet junkets from southern Canadian cities for a quick look, a bite of exotic local food, a stop at the souvenir stand, and back to the city, making minimum demands on remote areas. It is also predictable that more Europeans will make summer trips to Greenland for fishing and hiking.

As Natives become more confused by the instant media and more disturbed by intrusions, they may band together to present an even more unified front against rapid change, polarizing situations that have been dormant for a long time, and breeding an atmosphere for political discontent. There may be a return to a more traditional life as ethnic interest arises. (Maybe the dogs will defeat the snow machines in time!) This, coupled with a new burst of scientific interest, will lead to more archaeological work, including underwater investigations in Beringea.

Nobody doubts that there will be more planners in the north. The matter of waste disposal, housing, and health will be improved if the people demand it.

There will be offshore oil and gas drilling in the Beaufort and Chuckchi Seas in spite of dangers to northern ecology. Lease sales for these areas are scheduled for the late 1970's. Since the Soviet icebreaker *Arktika* broke through the ice to the North Pole in 1977 more activity from such ships is expected to help in resource transportation. Dome Petroleum, a Canadian corporation, is planning to build the world's first private icebreaker to lead specially strengthened tankers to move oil rigs, gas, and crude oil in and out of the icy seas. This is probably the first of such ships to enable corporations to work in spite of ice, although Canada may be sensitive to oil tankers from other nations in her arctic sector. More pipelines are on drawing boards now as governments and corporations plan for more oil and gas to be shipped.

The older generation of Native people contemplate the future with emotions as mixed as their living equipment.

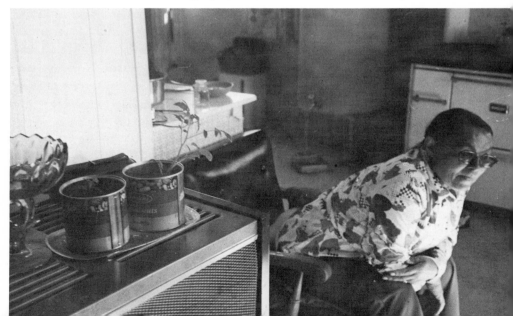

There are a number of international cooperative arctic research projects in progress or being planned for the 1980's decade. One of these in GISP, or Greenland Ice Sheet Program, a joint venture by Denmark, Switzerland, and the United States. Teams are at work to find out more about glaciers and their geophysical and thermal characterisitcs, and about the ancient climatic history of the ice cap. By making core borings, some to bedrock and below, scientists hope to reconstruct the nature, history, and origin of the ice sheet that will help global climatic predictions. There have been core borings in Greenland in the past, but this is the most extensive study to date. There are many related areas in the project, such as surface or sound studies at a dozen or so sites. The National Science Foundation supervises the United States' share of the work, part of which is done by CRREL, the Army's Cold Regions Research and Engineering Laboratory.

Investigators from England, Denmark, and the United States are planning project MIZ, Marginal Ice Zone, to study the effect of waves on ice floes. CANBARX, a Canadian and United States project, will study acoustics of the water, to learn more of how sound travels under water. The Nansen Drift Station is a proposed project to repeat the journey of Nansen's *Fram* for oceanographic study. It will include teams from Norway, Iceland, Sweden, Denmark, and the United States. The Canadian government has asked the United States to take part in their Lomonosov project, a plan to establish three floating camps near the North Pole to drift across the Lomonosov Ridge to learn more about undersea magnetic and seismic factors of the area. This project will work along with the FRAM project, a drift study planned by Norway, Canada, Denmark, and the United States. Norway plans a Coastal Dynamics study and a study of the permanent open water north of Spitsbergen, with other nations participating.

Some metering devices will be placed beneath the sea ice near Greenland in project East Greenland Drift. Norwegians and Americans will try there to learn more about the heat exchange in the East Greenland current that affects the ice conditions of the Arctic Ocean.

One proposal with a sentimental touch that all nations will

New construction for University of Tromsö, Norway, above the Arctic Circle

Norwegian scientists study causes and effects of the aurora borealis with sophisticated equipment at Auroral Institute in Tromsö.

watch with interest in YMER 79. It will be a circumpolar trip in a Swedish icebreaker to commemorate Adolf Erik Nordenskjöld's successful venture of 1879 when he took the *Vega* through the Northeast Passage, the first person to have done so.

The United States has a number of ongoing arctic research programs, mostly done by thirteen different agencies. Their works are coordinated under the Interagency Arctic Research Coordinating Committee of the National Science Foundation. Projects are reported in the *Arctic Bulletin* which can be had from the Polar Information Service, National Science Foundation, Washington, D.C., 20550. The various agency projects, mostly concerning Alaska, deal with space, energy, environmental protection, transportation, weather forecasting, conservation, game management and wildlife, health, and other matters appropriate to the agency involved. The National Science Foundation, Division of Polar Programs, provides research opportunities for qualified people with original thoughts about oceanography, glaciology, biology, meteorology and the like. The NSF provides a booklet, *Grants for Scientific Research,* which gives instructions on how to get a study grant.

The military establishments of all the arctic countries have bases, do research, and keep a close eye on the crown of the world. Their projects are not always made public, but one unclassified United States Navy scheme is intriguing enough for science fiction; Project MUMMERS (Manned-Unmanned Multipurpose Arctic Environmental Research Stations), a drift experiment, grew indirectly out of T-3, Fletcher's Ice Island. T-3 is still moving around the arctic, and in 1978 was put back into service as part of this new project. Other drift stations had been put to use in the arctic for research, but nothing as grand as MUMMERS. The idea is that many floes and ice islands will be set into drift patterns throughout the arctic, each equipped with Arctic Environmental Buoys. An AEB is a self-contained unmanned telemetry station to transmit data and can be installed in pack ice with a battery supply to last fourteen months. AEB's can monitor atmospheric pressure and temperature and show the position of the floe. Also the floating ice body will contain a Synoptic Random Access Measurement System, or SYNRAMS, which will record underwater noise, barometric pressure, and air temperature. The AEB's are controlled by shore-based radio, and the SYNRAMS relays its data to a satellite terminal point via a NIMBUS F Satellite.

Not only will MUMMERS have electronic devices out in the cold gathering constant information but they will be equipped to take care of people who wish to do several weeks of research on the spot when the temperature permits.

With a number of nuclear submarines operating in the arctic, the United States Navy has need for constant information. The Navy has recently turned over her huge petroleum reservation in Alaska to the Department of the Interior, and the likelihood is that the Navy Arctic Research Laboratory at Point Barrow, Alaska, will in the near future become a general federal research unit.

Modern arctic construction at Auyuittuq National Park Headquarters at Pangnirtung on Baffin Island, as man conquers the Arctic

It would seem that Man has conquered the arctic, doing everything there that a human mind could dream of, unmasking all the mysteries of the crown of the world, filling the waters with gimmicks, racing to the North Pole with flags held high, disturbing the animals and the Native people. But each generation has to conquer it again, for just as the supply of icebergs is constantly renewed, so is the human spirit of new generations who continue to respond to the Polar Star.

13

Are We Facing a New Ice Age?

++

When we put aside our packs and settled in to a Vermont winter, with snow piling up against the windows, one of the questions about the arctic was still not answered.

"Are we going into another ice age?" friends asked us eagerly, expecting us to know all about this matter that is puzzling scientists throughout the world. Our guess, from what we had seen and learned, was that the world is inevitably headed for another big ice sheet.

But to assure ourselves, we interviewed experts at the National Science Foundation in Washington, D.C., and at the United States Army Corps of Engineers Cold Regions Research and Engineering Laboratory (CRREL) at Hanover, New Hampshire. We steeped ourselves further in learned reports and then set about writing "Chapter Thirteen" as an ominous last word.

The answer we got from our scientific investigation was that yes, we probably are facing a cooling period and increasing glaciation in the world. If the northern hemisphere is once again to be host to a great ice sheet, nobody will risk setting a date, but it is agreed that maximum ice conditions will develop slowly. It certainly will not reach Vermont before we have worn out the handsome warm parkas we bought from the Canadian Inuit.

++

THE WORLD is growing colder and the trend will continue. That is the consensus of the best scientific predictions. Most climatologists hasten to hedge that statement by admitting that we do not

The ice increases as the world grows colder.

as yet have the technical ability to make positive and accurate climatic forecasts. But the ice is increasing. All it takes to make a new ice age is for the snow to fall faster than it melts for a number of years.

New knowledge of the earth's geological history shows climatic trends from the last millenia that can be used for reasonable assumptions about the future. Columns of earth, ice, and rock, called core samples, have been taken from several areas of ocean bottom and the Greenland ice cap by deep drilling.

These cores contain layers of fossils, plant remains, volcanic dust, and other debris from the past that can be removed to laboratories and studied by geologists, oceanographers, biologists, and other scientists. By putting together the knowledge gleaned from several cores there is now a picture of the earth's climate for the last 870,000 years or so.

By special techniques, experts have found in the layers of the cores the amount of oxygen that was present at a given time. Heavy oxygen, which has been detected in marine fossils and ice samples, is a sign of cold conditions, and a lack of heavy oxygen shows that the world was warmer at that period.

It has been known for a long time that there were recurring periods of glaciation in the world; the land bridge of Beringea appeared in cold periods when the water was tied up in glaciers, and went away when melting caused it to be flooded at least four times. Now, with new knowledge and new laboratory techniques, researchers believe there may have been some twenty ice ages with warming periods in between. The warm periods, according to the core studies, seem to have been shorter than the ice ages.

So, say some authorities, the cold world is the normal world, and the warming period in which we are living is the abnormal situation. It appears that we are nearing the end of the warming period and are returning to normal cold. The world seems to have been in the present warming period for the last six thousand years or more, which is the longest warming period yet discovered. This six thousand years is a mere blip on the earth's climate record.

Weather is a state of the atmosphere at a given time and is described by temperature, moisture, wind velocity, and air pressure. Climate is the trend and the sum of these meteorological conditions over a long period of time. We can have warm weather in a cold climate, but one session of warm weather does not change a cold climate. It could be argued on a very large scale that our years of warm weather did not change the cold climate of the earth.

There have been increasing warnings in the last five hundred years, in spite of some quite warm seasons, that the world's present warming period is coming to an end. Probably the first sign was the Little Ice Age from about 1450 to 1850 when historically the world is known to have been much colder.

Greenland, which is often suspected of being the world's climate indicator, became so cold in the early fifteenth century that the thriving Viking colonies there disappeared, partially due to the increasing ice in the northern seas that prevented ships from bringing the customary supplies from Europe. Less than a century later, people froze and starved from crop failures in Iceland and northern Europe. In 1816 many New England states and neighboring Canada had snow in every one of the twelve months of that year. In the 1970's parts of Baffin Island in Canada failed to have the ususal ice-free period in the summer. Unusual blizzards across the United States and Europe in the 1970's have left havoc and destruction.

While fearful cold strikes in the north, an equally fearful disaster is happening further south. The rising arctic cold is affecting the amount of moisture in other parts of the world, causing new desert areas in Africa, for example. The connection is that as more water turns to ice, there is less water in the air to be carried by the great winds that are constantly exchanging warm and cool air and providing moisture by condensation. Dryer winds mean that once fertile countries can become deathly deserts where no crops can grow.

Most people alive today have lived in a generally balmy world, even though without suspecting it we might have been in a long-range slide toward a colder world. Since 1900 the world has been warm enough to allow longer growing periods in England and Iceland. There are even tobacco plantations in New England, a thing unheard of in 1900. So it is with shock, if not outright resentment, that the climate-change prediction is received. Most people have cheerfully thought the cold winters recorded in colonial America would not come again. Benign climate would keep food supplies abundant and our only concern might be population that rises with good weather and plenty of food.

But these happy trends are reversing. Dr. Anthony J. Gow, a research geologist at CRREL, reports that the average temperature at the surface of the earth in the Northern Hemisphere has dropped about a half a degree centigrade since 1940. That sounds quite insignificant, but Dr. Gow feels that a further three- or four-degree decrease would see us in the midst of major glaciation with ice creeping into the United States and Europe in the pattern of the last great ice sheet.

Of course there are a few scientists who disagree and predict that the world is not going to glaciate further but could in fact get warmer. This minority group is not convinced that relying on earth's history is a valid means of predicting future climates. They argue that while some glaciers are indeed growing, there are others that show some annual decrease.

One of the things that all climatologists are aware of is that

Arctic sky and land

people themselves contribute to making the world warmer. Much of the world's heat is controlled by reflection and absorptions of the sun's rays. For extreme examples, ice reflects heat while concrete and desert lands absorb heat. The word "albedo," often used by climatologists, simply stated means the proportion of the amount of sunlight received to the amount of sunlight reflected back. In a roundabout way, human beings have some control over the earth's heat by disturbing the albedo.

One of the ways that humans have made the world warmer is by putting quantities of carbon dioxide into the air. Since about 1860 the world has been burning increasing amounts of coal, oil, and gas, for industrial purposes and for heating houses. Some, but not all, of this carbon dioxide is absorbed by the oceans, but there is such an abundance of it that the excess lies in a layer over the earth and produces a slight barrier.

The heat of the sun can come through this barrier to reach the earth, but the heat that would normally reflect back into space is partially trapped and returns to the earth to cause a secondary heating, sometimes called "the greenhouse effect." A few people have hopeful thoughts that this umbrella will delay, if not stop, the cooling tendency of the earth.

But people also can make the world cooler. When green growth is removed to allow erosion, the earth can become a desert, making dust that rises into the air and filters out the sun's rays, making the earth cooler. According to some experts, it is believed that dust can seed clouds that cut off energy from the sun. Contrails from jet planes make clouds too. All aerosols, that is, particles dispersed into the air in gas, can cut off the sun's heat. (Aerosols are not just spray bottles to aim at hair or bugs.)

Nature adds to the airborne debris with volcanic dust that can also block sunlight. When nature and man combine their activities, the results are often frightful. When clean fog, which can be a cooling and soothing blessing, mixes with industrial smoke, dust, carbon monoxide from automobile exhausts, and other foreign particles in the air, the result is smog, which can cut off the sun and cool the earth in an especially deadly fashion.

Oceans are important because they absorb heat and act as reservoirs to moderate climate. Yet in the icy Arctic Ocean there is a special natural condition. The polar ice pack, like all ice, reflects rather than absorbs heat from the sun, making the atmosphere colder. The more ice there is, the colder it gets, and that in turn makes more ice on the land and sea. Glaciers grow and the heat-absorbing water surface diminishes as the ocean becomes further covered with ice. This is how ice ages develop.

But what causes the cooling in the first place, and how does a warming period ever emerge in such a situation? There have been many theories but the most plausible and most widely accepted answer is the Milankovitch Hypothesis, developed in the 1930's by Milutin Milankovitch, from Yugoslavia, and Alfred Wegener, from Germany. Their conclusion was that the earth changes its attitude and orbit in relation to the sun, with the result that heat at the poles changes, causing ice sheets to come and go. The earth is said to wobble a bit in its orbit, causing these heat changes at the poles that trigger and end ice ages.

*The snow never melts, even on this midsummer day in northern
Greenland.*

The effects of ice ages are staggering, and some people have
thought that modern technology might be able to intervene and
stop them. A few years ago the Soviets proposed an idea to melt
the polar ice pack with nuclear power in order to improve shipping into Siberia. The results, it was quickly realized, would
mean flooding that would destroy New York, San Francisco,
London, Paris, Tokyo, and Leningrad. The few times that man
has tried to tamper with the climate have had serious side effects.
Experiments at seeding clouds to make rain triggered such
weather havoc that the efforts have been almost totally stopped.

Nature's Little Ice Age of a few hundred years ago caused
political and economic patterns that still haunt us. One of them
was the Irish potato famine in the middle of the nineteenth century. It was so cold and wet in Ireland that a special cold weather
blight attacked the potatoes, a fungus that would not have survived if the weather had been warmer. Thousands of Irish people

starved. The numbers of Irish who emigrated to America made economic changes far beyond their own country.

The serious cold conditions that ruined New England hill farms in the same period brought on an exodus of New Englanders who looked for a better life in the west. The recent famines in Africa, due to changes in the arctic ice, have brought death and destruction. If the United States, which is the most productive farm country in the world, suffers serious temperature changes, then it can no longer export food to less fortunate countries.

In the 1970's the Soviet Union had a wheat failure due to chilling effects. The resulting wheat purchases put the rest of the world in short supply and set up a chain reaction of political and economic results. Alterations in the world money market as the result of massive food purchases can affect inflation. There is no end to the importance of the arctic climate, which is controlled to a great degree by the amount of ice at the crown of the world.

What will we do if we have an ice sheet that again covers part of Canada and the United States and puts North America in walking distance of Asia once more? We can look back to the early people who came over the Bering land bridge and stayed in the north, living with cold, living on sea creatures and such land animals that can survive in a frigid climate. All the necessary food elements are present in the sea, and people have demonstrated that they can live with extreme cold. Polar Eskimos lived on the ice itself. Even our Pilgrim forefathers lived in houses that probably did not get much above freezing point in winter.

If the human race is not so stupid as to ruin the oceans or kill off the whales and seals and other creatures necessary for human survival, and will face the idea of a colder world with less food, and if nations will learn to cooperate, then there is hope for the future of human beings on earth.

Additional Reading

This list is intended only for more detailed reading suggestions, chiefly on current arctic matters, and does not represent a complete bibliography for CROWN OF THE WORLD.

Alexander, Colin. *Angry Society*. Yellowknife, NWT: Yellowknife Publishing Co., Ltd., 1976.

Armstrong, Terence/Roberts, Brian/Swithinbank, Charles. *Illustrated Glossary of Snow and Ice*. Cambridge: Scott Polar Research Institute, 1969.

Arnold, Robert D., et al. *Alaska Native Land Claims*. Anchorage: Alaska Native Claims Foundation, 1976.

Balikci, Asen. *The Netsilik Eskimo*. Garden City, N.Y.: Natural History Press, 1970.

Bank, Ted II. *People of the Bering Sea*. New York: MSS Educational Publishing Co., Inc., 1971.

Berry, Mary Clay. *The Alaska Pipeline*. Bloomington and London: Indiana University Press, 1975.

Bruemmer, Fred. *The Arctic*. Montreal: Infocor, Ltd., 1974.

Conolly, Violet. *Siberia Today and Tomorrow*. London and Glasgow: Collins, 1975.

Crowe, Keith J. *A History of the Original People of Northern Canada*. Montreal: Arctic Institute of North America, 1974.

Dall, William H. *Alaska and Its Resources*. New York: Arno and *The New York Times*, 1970 (reprint from 1870).

De Poncins, Gontran. *Kabloona*. New York: Reynal and Hitchcock, Inc., 1941.

Dyson, James L. *The World of Ice*. New York: Alfred A. Knopf, 1969.

Eames, Hugh. *Winner Lose All, Dr. Cook and the Theft of the North Pole*. Boston: Little, Brown, 1973.

Eidheim, Harald. *Aspects of the Lappish Minority Situation*. Oslo, Bergen, Tromsö: Universitetsforleget, 1974.

Erngaard, Erik. *Greenland Then and Now*. Copenhagen: Lademann, 1972.

Freuchen, Peter, and Salomonsen, Finn. *The Arctic Year*. New York: G. P. Putnam's Sons, 1958.

Fristrup, Borge. *The Greenland Ice Cap.* Copenhagen: Rhodos, 1966.

Gallagher, H. G. *Etok: A Story of Eskimo Power.* New York: G. P. Putnam's Sons, 1974.

Giddings, J. Louis. *Ancient Men of the Arctic.* New York: Alfred A. Knopf, 1973.

Golder, F. A. *Bering's Voyages.* New York: American Geographical Society, 1922.

Graburn, Nelson H. H., and Strong, B. Stephen. *Circumpolar Peoples: An Anthropological Perspective.* Pacific Palisades, Calif.: Goodyear Publishing Co. Inc., 1973.

Greve, Tim. *Svalbard, Norway in the Arctic.* Oslo: Grøndahl and Sons, 1975.

Gvozdetsky, N. A. *Soviet Geographical Explorations.* Moscow: Progress Publishers, 1977.

Hopkins, David M. *The Bering Land Bridge.* Stanford: Stanford University Press, 1967.

Ingold, Tim. *The Skolt Lapps Today.* Cambridge: Cambridge University Press, 1976.

Jones, Gwyn. *A History of the Vikings.* London: Oxford University Press, 1973.

Loomis, Chauncey C. *Weird and Tragic Shores.* New York: Alfred Knopf, 1971.

McCracken, David R. *Pipeline on the Permafrost.* Deer Lodge, Montana: Platen Press, 1976.

MacDonald, Edwin A. *Polar Operations.* Annapolis: US Naval Institute, 1969.

Manker, Ernst. *People of Eight Seasons.* Gothenburg: Ab Nordbok, 1975.

Malaurie, Jean. *The Last Kings of Thule.* (Translated from the French by Gwendolen Freeman) London: George Allen and Unwin, Ltd., 1956.

Mirski, Jeanette. *To the North!* New York: The Viking Press, 1934.

Mountfield, David. *A History of Polar Exploration.* London: Hamlyn, 1974.

Neatby, L. H. *Conquest of the Last Frontier.* Athens: Ohio University Press, 1966.

Neatby, L. H. *Discovery in Russian and Siberian Waters.* Athens: Ohio University Press, 1973.

Peary, Robert E. *The North Pole.* New York: Frederick Stokes, 1910.

Pelto, Pertti J. *The Snowmobile Revolution: Technology and Social Change in the Arctic.* Menlo Park, Calif.: Cummings Publishing Co., 1973.

Pimlott, Douglas/Brown, Dougald/Sam, Kenneth. *Offshore Drilling in the Canadian Arctic.* Ottawa: Canadian Arctic Resources Committee, 1976.

Rohmer, Richard. *The Arctic Imperative.* Toronto: McClelland and Stewart, 1975.

Rondière, Pierre. *Siberia Land of Promise.* (Adapted from a translation by Charles Duff) London: Constable, 1966.

Rudenko, S. I. *The Ancient Culture of the Bering Sea and the Eskimo Problem.* (Translated from Russian by Paul Tolstoy. Ed. by H. N. Michael) Toronto: University of Toronto Press, 1961.

Ruong, Israel. *The Lapps in Sweden.* Stockholm: The Swedish Institute for Cultural Relations with Foreign Countries, 1967.

Sater, John E. *The Arctic Basin.* Washington: Arctic Institute of North America, 1969.

Shinkarev, Leonid. *The Land Beyond the Mountains, Siberia and Its People Today.* New York: Macmillan, 1973.

Spencer, Robert F. *The North Alaskan Eskimo.* Washington: The Smithsonian Institution, 1959.

Stefansson, Vilhjamur. *Arctic Manual.* New York: Macmillan, 1944.

Stonehouse, Bernard. *Animals of the Arctic.* Great Britain: Peter Lowe, 1971.

Stuart, Frank S. *A Seal's World.* New York: Pyramid Communications by arrangement with Curtis Brown, 1954.

Valentine, Victor F., and Vallee, Frank G. *Eskimo of the Canadian Arctic.* Toronto: McClelland and Stewart, 1968.

Wickersham, James. *Old Yukon.* St. Paul, Minn.: West, 1938.

Wilkinson, Douglas. *Land of the Long Day.* Toronto: Clarke, Irwin and Co., 1955.

Wilkinson, Douglas. *The Arctic Coast.* Toronto: Natural Science of Canada, Ltd., 1975.

Wilson, Roger (editor). *The Land That Never Melts, Auyuittuq National Park.* Canada: Peter Martin Associates Ltd. in association with Parks Canada.

Explorers, Adventurers, and Wanderers: A Partial Chronology of People in the Arctic

Approximate Dates: (A.D. unless otherwise indicated)	Who and Why	Where, What, and Comments
23,000 to 28,000 B.C.	Asian Caucasoids, possibly related to the Ainus of Hokkaido, Japan, following game to north and east, and moving away from the pressures of aggressive Mongoloids	Crossed the then exposed Bering land bridge from Asia to Alaska, moving south as ice conditions permitted; these are the ancestors of the Indians of North and South America.
20,000 to 10,000 B.C.	Asian Mongoloids, possibly from Tibet, Mongolia, or China, following game	Moved by way of the valleys of the Amur and Anadyr Rivers of Siberia, then across the Bering land bridge into Alaska, and north and east, in waves now called Sarquaq, Dorset, and Thule cultures, across the Canadian arctic to Greenland. Also, these people moved west along the Siberian arctic coast to the mouth of the Kolyma River.
12,000 to 5,000 B.C.	Ancestors of the Yakuts, Yukagirs, Evens, Evenks, Nenets, Komi, Dolgans, Ngansans; some Caucasoids; some Mongoloids; taking advantage of a warming climate and receding ice to move into new lands	Some settled within the tree line in the taiga of north Siberia, some went on north into the tundra and arctic seacoast.
12,000 to 2,000 B.C.	Lapps (Samer) people, some of whom were Caucasoid, some Mongoloid, apparently from Central Russia, under pressure from aggressive neighbors	Moved north and west, dividing and adapting their lives as the sea, forest, and reindeer Lapps of Northern Scandinavia and the Soviet Union.

Approximate Dates:	Who and Why	Where, What, and Comments
2,500 B.C. (Possibly, in the light of recent discoveries, 28,000 B.C.)	Athapaskan Indians	Settled into Old Crow, on the Porcupine River, Yukon Territory, Canada, believed to be the oldest continuously occupied community in North America.
330 B.C.	Pytheas of Massilia (now Marseilles) in search for goods and markets	Sponsored by merchants, Pytheas sailed north via Scotland and the Hebrides to his "Thule," where the sun did not set in midsummer. An intriguing question: did the Scots tell him about the far north, and, if so, when had they gone there?
400 A.D.	Saint Brendan the Navigator, seeking peace and quiet	From Ireland, north and west, possibly to the Faroe Islands, Iceland, Jan Mayen, Greenland . . . and North America?
400–600	Various groups of Irish monks, seeking seclusion	To Iceland, where they had long been settled before the first Viking arrived to disturb them in 870.
867	Rabna Floki, from Norway, seeking new lands to settle	Floki used ravens to locate land, and sailed along the north coast of Iceland, by Grimsey Island, and settled in the northwest fiords, from which Greenland is visible on a clear day.
875	Ottar (Othar, Othere) from Norway	Explored the coast of northern Norway, the Kola Peninsula of Russia, and the White Sea. His travels were recorded by King Alfred of Britain.
932	Gunnbjorn Ulf-Krakason, Norwegian/Icelandic Viking, investigating new lands west of Iceland	Gunnbjorn sighted the east coast of Greenland, probably near Kulusuk and Angmagssalik. He described islands or "skerries" which were likely ice islands or tabular bergs like T-3.
982	Eric the Red, Viking, outlawed from Iceland for murder	Eric sailed to the east coast of Greenland, then south and west, establishing two settlements. His wife, a convert to Christianity by his son Leif, built the first Christian church in Greenland near her home in Bratalid.

Approximate Dates:	Who and Why	Where, What, and Comments
990	Bjarni Herjolfsson, Viking, from Norway and Iceland, trying to join his father in the new Greenland colony	Was blown off course by bad storms, and repeatedly saw coasts of North American lands, possibly Ellesmere and Baffin Islands, Labrador, and points south. He did not like the looks of these lands and would not let any of his crew land. He later sold his ship to Leif Ericsson, along with his navigation notes and some of his crew members.
1,000 to 1,020	Leif Ericsson, Thorvald Ericsson, Thorfinn Karlsefni, and others, Vikings from Iceland and Greenland, searching for new lands to settle	Sailed into and explored new lands west of Greenland, including Ellesmere and Baffin Islands, Labrador, Newfoundland, and possibly points south.
April 21, 1135	Erling Sigvason, Bjarne Tortasson, and Eindrid Odsson, Vikings, for reasons unknown	Left their names and the date on a stone at 72°55'N, above Disko Bay, Greenland.
1360	Nicholas of Lynn, a monk, and a friend of Chaucer	Using an astrolabe to navigate, he sailed for Norway and "points farther north," making five trips, but all of his books and records have been lost.
1497	Giovanni Caboto (John Cabot), a Genoese like Columbus, sailing for the merchants of the port of Bristol, England	Greenland, Labrador, possibly islands north of Labrador, and Newfoundland. Cabot found only good fishing grounds, which did not interest his sponsors.
1500	Miguel and Gaspar Cortereal, Portuguese	Greenland and Newfoundland; they were lost on a second voyage to northern waters.
Before 1553	Unidentified Scots in Vardo, arctic Norway	In 1553, they warned Richard Chancellor of the hazards of navigating the White Sea north of Russia.
1553 to 1556	Richard Chancellor, Hugh Willoughby, and Steven Borough, English, sailing in search of a Northeast Passage to China; sponsored by Grand Pilot Sebastian Cabot, son of John Cabot	Willoughby and two ships lost on east coast of Lapland, remains were found following year by Russian fishermen. Chancellor went on to Kola Peninsula and White Sea, traveled by land to Moscow. Chancellor was drowned

Approximate Dates:	*Who and Why*	*Where, What, and Comments*
		on second trip but Borough survived and, in 1556, went to Novaya Zemlya and the Kara Sea.
1565	Oliver Brunel, Dutch, to establish trading post at Archangel to compete with Chancellor's Muscovy Company	Visited Archangel, the White Sea, and, traveling overland as an agent of the Russian Stroganov family, the Ob River.
1576–1578	Sir Martin Frobisher, English, former pirate with a jail record, later killed in battle, searching for a Northwest passage to China	Frobisher made three voyages to Baffin Island, was wounded in rear end by Eskimo arrow, captured some Eskimos to prove that he was near China by their Mongoloid features; found fool's gold and his sponsor was later jailed for fraud.
1580	Arthur Pet and Charles Jackman, English, in search of the Northeast Passage	Sailed into the Kara Sea north of Russia; Jackman was lost.
1584	Oliver Brunel, Dutch, in search of the Northeast Passage	Sailed east from Archangel into Kara Sea ice pack; later made three voyages for Denmark searching for lost colonies of Greenland.
1584–1587	John Davis, English, in search of the Northwest Passage, sponsored by the geographer John Dee and the Hakluyt family	Davis made three voyages, surveyed the east coast of Greenland and Baffin Bay north to above 72°N, was an outstanding seaman and navigator.
1594–1595	Willem Barents, Nai, and Tetgales, Dutch, in search of the Northeast Passage	Made two voyages into Kara Sea but were stopped each time by ice.
1596–1597	Barents, Ryp, and Heemskerck, Dutch, in search of the Northeast Passage	Sailed to Bear Island, Spitsbergen, to 79°49'N, then Heemskerck and Barents rounded northern tip of Novaya Zemlya, were iced in for winter, Barents dying in a small boat as they sailed toward the Kola Peninsula the following summer.
1602	George Weymouth (Waymouth), English, in search of the Northwest Passage	Greenland and the Davis Strait; forced to return to England by mutiny led by ship's chaplain.

Approximate Dates:	Who and Why	Where, What, and Comments
1603	James Cunningham, John Knight, James Hall, English, sponsored by the King of Denmark and Norway, in search of the lost colony of Greenland	West coast of Greenland; found silver which turned out to be lead; kidnapped two Eskimos who died in captivity.
1606	John Knight, English, in search of the Northwest Passage	Explored coasts of islands west of Greenland, then Labrador, where Knight was killed by Eskimos.
1605–1612	James Hall, three voyages in search of the Northwest Passage, the last with William Baffin as pilot	West coast of Greenland. On last voyage, Hall was recognized by a relative of an Eskimo he had kidnapped earlier and was killed.
1607–1611	Henry Hudson, English, sailing for Dutch or for English, on voyages in search of both the Northeast and Northwest passages	Greenland, Spitsbergen, 80°N, Jan Mayen, Hudson Bay, Hudson River, New York. On last voyage Hudson, one of England's finest navigators, was, with his son and some loyal crew, put adrift in a small boat and perished. Some of the mutineers had mutinied against Hudson on an earlier voyage. Five of the mutineers stopped on the way home at Cape Digges on Hudson Strait to bargain for meat and fresh sorrel and were attacked and killed by Eskimos. Mate Bylot, one of the mutineers, took the ship back to England, had no charges made against him, and left again the same year with Sir Thomas Button.
1607–1733	Numerous Dutch Whalers, including van Lambert, van Edam, Gael Hamke, Carolus and Danell	Numerous whaling voyages into the waters around Spitsbergen, and along the east coast of Greenland, from Angmagssalik north to 74°N.
1609–1614	Poole, Marmaduke, Baffin, and others, English, many voyages	Spitsbergen
1612–1613	Sir Thomas Button, English, with Robert Bylot, mutineer against Hudson, in search of Henry Hudson and the Northwest Passage	Two voyages into Hudson Bay, then west and north to Southampton Island

202

Approximate Dates:	Who and Why	Where, What, and Comments
1612–1616	William Baffin, five voyages (one with Robert Bylot as pilot) in search of the Northeast and Northwest passages	Spitsbergen, Greenland to north of 78°N, Baffin Bay and Hudson Bay
1631–1632	Luke Foxe (Northwest Foxe) and Thomas James, English, in search of the Northwest Passage	Foxe explored Hudson Strait, and west to Foxe Channel and Foxe Basin to 67°N. James, a poor seaman, ended up in James Bay below Hudson Bay but wrote a charming book and became a popular hero, while Foxe was ignored.
1648	Semeon (Simon) Dezhnev, Russian Cossack, tribute collector, in several small boats, then on foot after boats were wrecked	Traveled down Siberia's Kolyma River, around East Cape (now Cape Dezhnev) through Bering Strait to the Anadyr. Some authorities question the authenticity of this trip.
1707	Cornelius Giles, Dutch whaler	Discovered the easternmost island of the Spitsbergen/Svalbard group, now called Giles Land.
1721	Hans Egede, Danish minister, missionary, in search of the lost colonies of Greenland	West coast of Greenland
1725–1742	Russia's Great Northern Expedition, sponsored by Peter the Great, and later by Catherine; involved Vitus Bering, a Dane, Khariton Laptev, Dmitri Laptev, Chelyuskin, and others	Mapping and exploration of the north coast of Russia and Siberia, Bering Strait and Bering Sea, and the arctic rivers
1730	Shestakov and geodesist Gvosdev, on an expedition to subdue the Chuckchi of northeastern Siberia	After Shestakov had failed to subdue the Chuckchis and left his head on display in a village, Gvosdev, as the senior survivor, sailed to the Bering Strait and landed in Alaska.
1760–1762	Shalaurov, a merchant of Yakutsk, Siberia, with a crew of exiles, to sail around the East Cape	Sailed down the Lena River from Yakutsk, to the Yana River, and on to the Kolyma River. On their fourth attempt to reach the arctic sea, all disappeared.

203

Approximate Dates:	*Who and Why*	*Where, What, and Comments*
1769–1771	Samuel Hearne, of the Hudson Bay Company, to look for a river with banks of copper	Hearne, one of the first westerners to travel as the natives did, was helped by friendly Indians, who proceeded to massacre their traditional enemies, the Eskimos, at Bloody Falls on the Coppermine River. Hearne reached Coronation Gulf at the mouth of the Coppermine River.
1770–1773	Lyakhov, a Russian merchant, followed by other Russian traders looking for mammoth ivory; Sannikov, Byelkov, Sirovatsoi, and the surveyor, Hedenstrom	Lyakhov took a business trip to the Svyatoi Nos Peninsula, then two trips of exploration. In 1773 he and one other man rowed a boat out to the New Siberian Island named for him, spent the winter there, and found rich stores of mammoth ivory.
1773	Constantine Phipps, English, with fourteen-year-old midshipman Horatio Nelson as a boat coxswain	Explored waters around Spitsbergen, where, on two occasions, Horatio Nelson was reported to have driven off attacks on other small boats by a walrus and a bear.
1778	James Cook, English, on his third voyage of discovery, accompanied, among others, by William Bligh, later the captain of the *Bounty*; Joseph Billings; and John Ledyard, American	Sailed and explored the coast of Alaska; Cook Inlet, near Anchorage being explored by Bligh in a small boat; contacted Russians at Unalaska, using the American Ledyard as liaison man; sailed north through the Bering Strait until stopped by ice above Icy Cape, near Barrow, Alaska.
1778–1787	John Ledyard, American, adventurer, traveler	Ledyard was born in Groton, Conn., briefly attended Dartmouth College, sailed with Captain Cook as a Corporal of the Marine Guard, later undertook to walk around the world, was arrested as a spy in northern Siberia, visited in 1787 in Yakutsk by his old shipmate Joseph Billings. Later Ledyard did walk through much of Lapland, and died in Egypt at the age of thirty-eight.
1779	Clerke (Clark, Clarke), English, ship captain under Captain James Cook, returned north after Cook was killed in Hawaii	Again attempted to go north of the Bering Strait, but was stopped by ice at the level of Point Barrow, Alaska. Clerke was dying from a disease he caught while in debtor's prison after he returned from an earlier voyage with Captain Cook.

Approximate Dates:	Who and Why	Where, What, and Comments
1787	Joseph Billings, English, assistant astronomer on Cook's Third Voyage, hired by Russian Empress Catherine to survey arctic coast of Siberia, from the Kolyma River to East Cape, by ship	Reached the mouth of the Kolyma River, then sailed east to Chaunskaya Bay where he was stopped by ice, returning to Yakutsk where he encountered Ledyard.
1789	Alexander Mackenzie, Scottish merchant for the Northwestern Fur Company	Explored the Mackenzie River, starting at Lake Athabaska, to Great Slave Lake, then to the mouth of the river on the Beaufort Sea. Later, in 1793, he traveled west across the Rocky Mountains to the mouth of the Bella Coola River in British Columbia, Canada.
1806–1813	Ludwig Giesecke, German mineralogist, actor, and reputed author of the libretto to Mozart's *Magic Flute*	Using an Eskimo boat, an umiak, Giesecke did a thorough mineral survey of all the known coast of Greenland, discovering, among other things, the deposits of cryolite, presently important to the Greenland economy.
1806–1822	William Scoresby and William Scoresby, Jr., English, whalers, observers, recorders, and leaders; in search of new whaling waters and information, numerous ship voyages, repeated experience with sea ice, mapping, and surveys	The Scoresbys made fourteen voyages into Greenland and Spitsbergen waters alone; they are responsible for the "crow's nest" for lookouts, for the ice drill, and for rocking a ship from side to side to free it from the ice by having the crew run from one side to another, known as "sallying" ship. In 1806 they reached 81°31′N; in 1822, they surveyed the east coast of Greenland.
1818	Two English expeditions, with members including Edward Parry, John Franklin, George Back, John Ross, Edward Sabine, James Clark Ross, and Buchan; in search of the Northwest Passage, and to sail to the North Pole, believed to lie in an unfrozen polar sea	Buchan and Franklin went north to N.W. Spitsbergen, using Phipps's chart, but were stopped by ice at Magdalen Bay; surveyed N.W. Spitsbergen. John Ross and Parry went to Baffin Bay, along west Greenland to Melville Bay, Cape York, observing "red snow" and "Arctic Highlander" Eskimos, later to help Peary as Etah, or Polar Eskimos. Ross started down Lancaster Sound, now known to be the beginning of the Northwest Passage, but turned back when

Approximate Dates:	*Who and Why*	*Where, What, and Comments*
		he saw land enclosing it; likely he saw a mirage, common at that latitude.
1819–1820	Edward Parry, English, with Sabine and Liddon, in search of the Northwest Passage	Parry, an excellent navigator and leader, used innovative means to keep expedition well and happy during winter, including publication of a newspaper, production of plays, and growing vegetables, to prevent scurvy, near ship's heating systems. He passed North Devon, Cornwallis and Bathurst islands, reached Melville Island, but was turned back at McClure Strait, beyond which lie the Beaufort Sea and Alaska.
1819–1822	John Franklin, George Back, Dr. John Richardson, aided by the Indian chief Akaitcho, to explore by land the arctic coastline east of the Coppermine River, surveyed by Hearne	Traveling by canoe, raft, and on foot, Franklin's party surveyed thousands of miles of river and coastal areas, suffering great hardships and problems, including cannibalism and the killing of the cannibal Michel by Richardson.
1820–1824	F. von Wrangell and Anjou, Russians, to survey the coast of Siberia from the Kolyma River east to East Cape (Cape Dezhnev) by land	Wrangell went east as far as Cape Yakan, below Wrangel Island, and made repeated sorties out on the sea ice in search of land; he learned from his native guides to use sastrugi, wind-driven snow ridges, as navigational aids.
1821–1825	Parry's second and third voyages, in search of the Northwest Passage south of McClure Strait	These voyages were unsuccessful insofar as the location of the Passage was concerned, but Parry, as usual innovative, learned to travel and to survive as the Eskimos did.
1823	Clavering and Sabine, English, to complete the pendulum observations Sabine had done earlier in Norway and Spitsbergen	Traveled by ship through the ice field off East Greenland north to 74°N, then by small boat to Shannon Island, finding a small Eskimo community at Gael Hamke's Bay, identified by description of that early Dutch whaler.
1825–1826	Beechey and Elson, English, in support of Parry and Franklin expeditions	Traveled by ship through the Bering Strait, north to Icy Cape; Elson then went by boat to Point Barrow, Alaska.

Approximate Dates:	*Who and Why*	*Where, What, and Comments*
1825–1827	Franklin, Back, Kendall, and Richardson, English, to descend the Mackenzie River and explore coast	Established Fort Franklin on Great Bear Lake, surveyed coastline west to Return Reef, and east to the mouth of the Coppermine River.
1827	Parry, English, to reach the North Pole	By ship, Parry traveled to North Spitsbergen, Treurenberg Bay; then, by foot, pulling sledges, which were boats with runners, over sea ice to 82°45′N where Parry realized that the ice was drifting south almost as fast as they could walk north.
1827	Keilhau, Swedish geologist	Geological survey of Spitsbergen
1829–1833	Sir John Ross, and his nephew, James Clark Ross, who served with Parry on three voyages, in search of the Northwest Passage, sponsored by gin distiller Booth, Sheriff of London	Used first steam-driven ship in the Arctic, exploring Lancaster Sound; James Clark Ross, in 1831, located the Magnetic North Pole on the Boothia Peninsula of Canada.
1833–1837	Sir George Back, English, in search of the Northwest Passage	Explored the Great Fish River, now called Back River, and areas west of Hudson Bay, Canada.
1837–1839	Dease and Simpson, Hudson Bay Company, to map the Arctic coastline	Traveled by boat to the mouth of the Mackenzie River; then Simpson, the younger of the two, went by umiak and on foot to Point Barrow, Alaska, then east to Victoria Island. Simpson, on a trip south to get mail, went mad, shot two companions, and died himself, by his own hand or by one of his companions'.
1837	Loven, Swedish geologist	Geological survey of the west coast of Spitsbergen
1845–1848	Sir John Franklin, English, in search of the Northwest Passage	Sailed from England to Disko Island, Greenland, into Lancaster Sound, Canada, by Cornwallis and Beechey islands, and was iced in near King William Land. Franklin died on board ship on June 11, 1847, at age 61. Ships were later abandoned in the ice and expedition tried to walk out but all hands died, the last near Point Ogle and Montreal Island.

Approximate Dates:	Who and Why	Where, What, and Comments
1846–1847	Dr. John Rae, English, of Hudson Bay Company, to complete survey started by Dease and Simpson, and possibly to meet Sir John Franklin	Rae, the first explorer really to depend on arctic food resources, surveyed Rae Inlet, Prince Regent Island, to Fury and Hekla Strait.
1848–1859	Numerous expeditions searching for Franklin, including: Kellett, 1848–1851 James Ross and McClintock, 1848–1849 Collison and McClure, 1850–1854 Rae, 1851 DeHaven and Dr. Kane, 1850–1851 Austin, Ommanney, John Ross, *et al*, 1850–1851 Kennedy and Bellot, 1851–1852 Inglefield, 1852 Belcher, McClintock, Kellett, *et al*, 1852–1854 Rae, 1853–1854 Kane, Hayes, and Hedrik, 1853–1855 Anderson, 1855 McClintock, Hobson, and Young, 1857–1859	Searches, many of which were instigated, sponsored, or inspired by Franklin's widow, resulted in much detailed exploration and mapping of the Canadian and Greenland arctic; a total of forty parties were reported. Rae, in 1854, found items from Franklin party in possession of Eskimos; Anderson of the Hudson Bay Company bought similar articles in 1855; in 1859, Hobson and McClintock found bodies, equipment, and a cairn left by Franklin party on the attempted march out.
1856	Lord Dufferin, English, owner and operator of a pleasure yacht	Cruised, for the fun of it, to Iceland, Jan Mayen, and Spitsbergen.
1858, and 1861	Two expeditions, led by Torrell and Nordenskjöld, Swedish geologists	Geological survey, Spitsbergen
1860–1861	Dr. Isaac Hayes, Sonntag, Americans, and Hans Hendrik, Greenland Eskimo	Measured the movements of glaciers on the edges of the Greenland ice cap; Sonntag died of exposure after falling through the ice; Hayes crossed Smith Sound and sledged up east coast of Ellesmere Island, Canada.
1860–1873	Charles Francis Hall, American, printer, age 40, from Cincinnati, three exploratory trips, the first nominally in	Hall lived as an Eskimo, learned their language, and found some supplemental information about the Franklin party. He died of

Approximate Dates:	Who and Why	Where, What, and Comments
	search of information about Franklin, the last to reach the North Pole	arsenic poisoning on his last trip and is buried at Thank God Harbor, northwest Greenland.
1863–1871	Elling Carlsen, Norwegian sealer, repeated voyages	Carlsen, in 1863, made first known circumnavigation of Spitsbergen. In 1871, at Ice Haven, Novaya Zemlya, he found Barents' house, letters, and books.
1864–1883	Nordenskjöld, Swedish, repeated expeditions	Surveyed and mapped northern Spitsbergen; attempted to reach North Pole, using reindeer; attempted to cross Greenland ice cap; and, in 1878–1879, made first ship trip through the Northeast Passage.
1865	James Waddell, American, in Confederate cruiser *Shenandoah*, raiding and capturing Union whalers and merchantmen.	The *Shenandoah* passed through the Bering Strait on June 29, 1865, and cruised north in the Chuckchi Sea until stopped by ice, then headed south intending to capture San Francisco, but was finally convinced that war had ended.
1867	Thomas Long, American whaler, hunting whales in Chuckchi Sea	Reported the discovery of "new" land, 500 miles north of Bering Strait, long known to natives of region: Wrangel Island.
1868–1871	Karl Koldeway and Hegemann, Germans, and Julius Payer, Austrian, several trips, in an attempt to reach the North Pole	Spitsbergen, Jan Mayen, Iceland, and the east coast of Greenland, sledging north as far as Cape Bismark, 77°N
1871–1874	Payer and Karl Weyprecht, Austrians, sponsored by German geographer Petermann, to follow branch of Gulf Stream north and find ice-free route to the North Pole and the Northeast Passage	Discovered Franz Josef Land.
1875–1877	Nares, Markham, and others, English, assisted by Hans Hendrik, Greenland Eskimo, and Petersen, Danish	Explored coasts of northwest Greenland and Ellesmere Island, and sledged on the frozen sea north to 83°20′N, and to Cape Columbia at northern tip of Ellesmere Island, Canada.

Approximate Dates:	Who and Why	Where, What, and Comments
1875–1876	Sir Allen Young, master of a vessel under McClintock in 1857–1859, attempted to navigate the Northwest Passage by yacht	Young was stopped by ice in Bellot Strait, near the De La Rouquette Islands.
1878–1879	Schwatka and Gilder, Americans, sponsored by the New York *Herald*, in search of more information on the Franklin expedition	By sledge to Back River, Simpson Strait, and King William Land
1879	Moirer and Wandel, Danish Navy	Made a survey of sea ice on the east coast of Greenland to 69°N.
1879–1882	Lt. De Long, U.S. Navy, in the ship *Jeanette*, in an attempt to reach the North Pole by ship to Wrangel Land, believed to be a part of an arctic continent, then by sledge to the Pole	The *Jeanette* was crushed in ice on June 12, 1881, and De Long and most of the expedition perished. Then survivors led by G. W. Melville, later an admiral, made their way across the ice to the mouth of the Lena River of Siberia.
1880–1881	Yachtsman Leigh Smith, attempting to find an ice-free route from Spitsbergen to Franz Josef Land	Smith's vessel was sunk by the ice, but her supplies were taken off and the party wintered over on Franz Josef and collected many specimens of flora and fauna.
1881–1884	Adolphus Greely, later a general, established and commanded a station at Lady Franklin Bay, Ellesmere Island, as part of the U.S. part in the International Polar Research Program; he also had instructions to try to reach the North Pole	Greely explored northwest Greenland and Ellesmere Island; support vessels failed to arrive, however, and only Greely and six others survived.
1882–1883	First International Circumpolar Year research stations	Austro-Hungary: Jan Mayen Denmark: Greenland and Kara Sea U.S.A.: Ellesmere I.; Pt. Barrow, Alaska Finland: Sodankyla Germany: Baffin Island Great Britain: Great Slave Lake, Canada Holland: Dickson, Yenesei R., Russia Norway: North Cape Russia: Lena Delta, Novaya Zemlya Sweden: Spitsbergen

Approximate Dates:	Who and Why	Where, What, and Comments
1882–1896	Fridtjof Nansen, Norwegian, repeated trips, voyages, and explorations	In 1882, Nansen collected plant specimens in East Greenland, and, in 1888 with Otto Sverdrup, crossed the Greenland ice cap. In 1893–1896, again with Sverdrup, he drifted in the specially built vessel *Fram* across the Arctic Ocean, duplicating the route followed by the wreckage of the *Jeanette* from Wrangel I. to Iceland. Nansen and one companion left the *Fram* at closest point to the Pole and attempted to sledge to the Pole but failed and were picked up by F. Jackson on Franz Josef Land; Sverdrup took the *Fram* through the rest of the drift and home to Norway.
1883	Charles Brower, George Leavitt, Americans, looking for coal deposits near Point Barrow, Alaska, for use by ships of Pacific Steam Whaling Company; plus others, before and after, involved in whaling in the Chuckchi and Beaufort Seas	Brower and Leavitt, whose descendants are leaders in the Barrow area, went north to prospect, but stayed, married, and prospered.
1891–1909	Robert E. Peary, civil engineer, U.S. Navy, the man who would not give up, five expeditions to explore northern Greenland and to reach the North Pole, accompanied at various times by Matthew Henson, his personal servant, and by Bob Bartlett, Dr. Frederick Cook, Donald MacMillan, George Borup, and others	Peary suffered a broken leg, lost part of one foot to frostbite, and barely survived many hardships, but finally reported reaching the North Pole on April 6, 1909. He, and his many influential supporters, later became involved in an acrimonious debate concerning the claim of Dr. Cook to have reached the Pole a year earlier. Henson was the only non-Eskimo to go all the way with Peary, Bartlett being sent back, having broken trail most of the way, to save provisions, at 87°47′N, 133 nautical miles from the Pole.
1894–1897	Frederick Jackson, English, sponsored by an English newspaper, to explore Franz Josef Land and find a route to the North Pole	Jackson explored Franz Josef Land and rescued Nansen and Johansen from Franz Josef, which they had reached after their attempt to reach the North Pole from the *Fram* in 1896.

211

Approximate Dates:	Who and Why	Where, What, and Comments
1896–1897	Sir Martin Conway, English, two expeditions	Spitsbergen, the first to cross the entire island, the second to survey areas of the north coast
1897	Salomon August Andree, Swedish scientist, and Strindberg and Fraenkel, to fly over the North Pole in a gas-filled free balloon	This party took off from Dane Island, Spitsbergen, on July 11, 1897; homing pigeons carrying messages regarding their progress were released periodically. One, landing on the mast of a Norwegian sealing vessel where it was shot for food, fell in the water and was abandoned. Later it was recovered when the captain learned from another ship that Andree was using pigeon messengers. Fog and ice brought balloon down after 65 hours at 82°56′N, 29°52′E. All three men died on White Island or Giles Land, near N.E. Spitsbergen. Their records and remains were found in 1930 by Dr. Gunnar Horn and Capt. Peder Eliassen, of a Norwegian expedition.
1898–1902	Otto Svedrup, Norwegian, who had accompanied Nansen on two expeditions, to explore North Greenland and other unknown areas; sponsored by consul Axel Heiberg, and the Ringnes brothers, brewers	Svedrup, again using the *Fram* in which he had drifted with Nansen, sailed to the west coast of Greenland, to Starvation Camp, where Greely had suffered; visited Peary, turned south and west through Jones Sound. Sledging trips west of Ellesmere Island discovered the Svedrup Islands, including those named for his sponsors, Axel Heiberg, Ellef Ringnes, and Amund Ringnes. His cartographer Isachsen left his name on a camp on Ellef Ringnes Island.
1899–1908	Numerous whaling ships operating in the Beaufort Sea off Alaska wintered over in the harbor of Canada's Herschel Island	Included Captain Klinkenberg of the *Olga* and Captain James Wing of the *Karluk*, later to be used by Stefansson. Whalers were looked on as potential sources of supplies by explorers.
1899–1900	Duke of Abruzzi, Italian North Polar Expedition, in search of a route to the Pole from Franz Josef Land	Lt. Cagni, Italian Navy, sledged north for 45 days, after the Duke was disabled by the loss of part of his hand from frostbite; Cagni reached a point 22 miles north of Nansen's northermost point.

Approximate Dates:	Who and Why	Where, What, and Comments
1900	Lt. G. Amdrup, Swedish Army, with Mikkelsen, Lt. J. P. Koch, and others, to survey east coast of Greenland; sponsored by foundation of the Carlsberg Brewers	Surveyed eastern Greenland north to Cape Bismark.
1903–1906	Roald Amundsen, Norwegian, in the small herring boat *Gjoa*, in search of the Northwest Passage	Sailed from east to west through the Northwest Passage for the first time, wintering over for two winters at Gjoa Haven, then sailing through Cambridge Bay below Victoria Island and Banks Island, spending a third winter off the mouth of the Mackenzie River at King Point near Herschel Island, then sailing on to Point Barrow and Nome, Alaska, where they arrived on August 31, 1906.
1906–1908	Mylius Erichsen, J. P. Koch, Trolle, Hagen, Wegener, and, as a stoker, student Peter Freuchen, sponsored by the Danish government and the Carlsberg Foundation to survey the east coast of Greenland	Two survey parties covered the coastline north of Cape Bismark to Peary Land at 82°37′N. Hagen, Erichsen, and the Eskimo Bronlund perished, but diaries and Hagen's maps were found with the body of Bronlund, the last to die. The bodies of Hagen and Erichsen were found by Mikkelsen, 1909–1912.
1906–1918	Vilhjalmur Stefansson, born in Canada of Icelandic parents, American, exploring and surveying areas of the arctic regions of Canada, accompanied by many, including, on his last expedition in the whaler *Karluk*, Bob Bartlett, who had almost reached the Pole with Peary, and anthropologist Diamond Jenness	Several expeditions, one of five years, living and traveling as an Eskimo, Stefansson becoming so adept at survival that he described the arctic as "friendly." He discovered new lands including Meighen, Brock, Borden and Lougheed islands, and the Horton River, drifting past Old Crow on the Porcupine River in 1907 and meeting Amundsen in the *Gjoa* at Herschel Island in 1906. His last expedition in the *Karluk* resulted in some loss of life when the ship was crushed in the ice after he had departed on a sledging trip, and survivors were brought out with help obtained by Bartlett.
1906–1907	Ernest de Koven Leffingwell, American, and Ejnar Mikkelsen, Danish, to conduct	The ship in which the party was traveling was stopped by ice conditions along the north coast of

	ethnological study of the Eskimos of Victoria Island, with Stefansson as a part of the original party who came down the Mackenzie River, barely making contact with the main group	Alaska. Leffingwell is credited with the idea of using a greased canvas bottom to convert a sledge to a boat for crossing leads in the ice pack.
1907–1909	Dr. Frederick Cook, American, who had been part of Peary's 1891–1892 expedition, and who had resigned from Peary's 1893 expedition because of Peary's contract provisions as to lectures and writings, nominally on a hunting trip, which became an attempt to sledge from Greenland to the North Pole	Cook claimed to have sledged some 4000 miles, and to have reached the North Pole on April 21, 1908, a year before Peary, then wintering over on a small island near Ellesmere Island. Doubts were cast on this accomplishment, and photographs were questioned that showed Eskimos at the Pole dressed in skins of animals reported killed after the Pole had been visited. The relative merits of Cook and Peary continue to be debated to the present time.
1909–1912	Ejnar Mikkelsen, Danish, with Laub, Jorgensen, and Iversen, in the ship *Alabama*, to search in N.E. Greenland for the bodies and diaries of Erichsen and Hagen	The bodies and records were located and recovered, and Erichsen's geographical findings were verified.
1912–1924	Knud Rasmussen, half Danish, half Eskimo, several exploratory and anthropological expeditions in Greenland, Canada, Alaska, and Siberia, accompanied at various times by Peter Freuchen, Lauge Koch, nephew of J. P. Koch, Thirkel Mathiassen, Kaj Birket-Smith, and Helge Bangsted	Rasmussen crossed the ice cap of Greenland, established, with Freuchen, trading post at Thule, conducted studies of the central Canadian arctic peoples, and, accompanied by two Eskimos, sledged from Greenland to East Siberia, conducting ethnological studies en route.
1912	Quervain, Swiss	Crossed Greenland ice cap, Disko to Angmagssalik.
1912–1913	J. P. Koch, Danish, and Alfred Wegener, German, using horses, to investigate atmospheric and glaciological conditions in the interior of Greenland	Some horses died, some ran away, some were eaten, but the men survived and reached the coast after spending a winter on the interior ice.

214

Approximate Dates:	Who and Why	Where, What, and Comments
1913–1915	Commander Vilkitski, Russian Navy, to make a hydrographic survey of the Northeast Passage from east to west	Using two icebreakers, and wintering over in Petropavlovsk, he completed the voyage in 1915.
1913–1917	Donald B. MacMillan, American, who had accompanied Peary on his final Polar expedition, and who sailed in and explored subarctic waters on many voyages, to explore "Crocker Land," reported by Peary north of Ellesmere Island	MacMillan saw "Crocker Land" but believed it to be a mirage which appeared and disappeared periodically. Some present scientists believe it could have been a tabular berg from an Ellesmere glacier, the birthplace of ice island T-3. MacMillan mapped Axel Heiberg, the Ringnes Islands and King Christian Land.
1914	Unidentified Russian aviators, prior to the establishment of the Soviet Union, hence not part of the Soviet arctic history	Conducted the first arctic survey flights along the north coast of Russia and Siberia.
1920–1923	Lauge Koch, Danish, leading the Danish Bicentenary Jubilee Expedition	Explored North Greenland, from Inglefield Gulf, Fort Conger, De-Long Fjord, to J. P. Koch's old camp at Cape Bridgman.
1924	Prof. George Binney, English Oxford Expedition to Spitsbergen	Several flights over Spitsbergen and N.E. Land, aircraft were finally wrecked and abandoned.
1924–1925	Richard E. Byrd, U.S. Navy, and Donald B. MacMillan, Americans	In connection with MacMillan's expedition to Etah, Greenland, several survey flights were made, but flying was severely restricted by weather.
1925	Roald Amundsen, Norwegian, and Lincoln Ellsworth, American, in an attempt to fly from Spitsbergen to the North Pole	Using two flying boats, they got within 100 miles of the Pole, landing there in a lead of open water, one plane being wrecked in the process. The party, packed into the remaining plane, finally got into the air four weeks later, but was forced down north of Spitsbergen, taxied, and was finally towed to land.
1926	Richard E. Byrd, American	Flew to North Pole and back from Spitsbergen.

215

Approximate Dates:	Who and Why	Where, What, and Comments
1926	Amundsen, Ellsworth, and General Umberto Nobile, in the airship *Norge*, piloted and designed by Nobile	Using the same base in Spitsbergen as Byrd, King's Bay, the *Norge* crossed the Arctic Ocean, via the Pole, to a settlement near Nome, Alaska.
1927–1928	Hubert Wilkins, Australian, and Carl Ben Eilson, American	Made several short polar flights, including one of the first ice landings to repair a mechanical problem, take off again, then later crash on the ice 70 miles off Barrow to which they walked. In 1928, they flew from Alaska to Spitsbergen via the Pole. Eilson was later lost while trying to fly out a cargo of furs from the ship *Nanook* in Siberian waters.
1928	General Nobile, Italian, in a second airship, *Italia*, backed by Mussolini's government of Italy	Flying from Spitsbergen, Nobile reached the Pole but the airship iced up and crashed. The survivors were finally rescued from the ice, 180 miles north of King's Bay, by a Swedish army pilot and by the Soviet icebreaker *Krassin*.
1928	Lt. Einar Lundborg, and Lt. Schiberd, Swedish army pilots	Lundborg made an ice landing, rescued Nobile, but crashed on his second landing. Schiberd made a second successful ice landing, rescued Lundborg, but deterioration of the ice prevented further landings.
1928	Roald Amundsen, in a French aircraft, with Guilbard, Dietrichsen, Valette, and Brazy, in search of Nobile's party	Amundsen and aircraft crew were lost over the Barents Sea searching for the *Italia*.
1930–1931	British Arctic Air Route Expedition, to investigate possible air routes from England to Canada via the Faroe Islands, Iceland, Greenland, Baffin Island, and Hudson Bay, led by Gino Watkins, age 23	The expedition made air surveys and took photos of the east coast of Greenland, and one member, Courtauld, spent five months alone in a tent on the ice cap taking weather observations. Watkins, a gifted leader, returned to Greenland in 1932 and was killed in a kayak accident.
1930	Alfred Wegener, German, on his third trip to the Greenland ice cap, to study	Wegener, who originated the theory of continental drift, was, with two Greenlanders, killed on

Approximate Dates:	Who and Why	Where, What, and Comments
	climatic conditions and measure the thickness of the ice cap	the ice cap. His continental drift theory was advocated and expanded by the Yugoslav Milankovich, along with theories as to the causes of ice ages.
1930–1932	Ushakov, Soviet, and three companions surveyed "Lenin Land," now known as Northern Land, by icebreaker *Georgi Sedov* to Domashny Island, then onward by sledge	Ushakov and companions sledged to and mapped four of the larger islands of Northern Land, plus several smaller ones.
1932	Sir Hubert Wilkins, Australian, in an attempt to reach the North Pole by submarine	Wilkins, using on old U.S. Navy submarine rented for $5.00 per year, renamed the *Nautilus*, went under the ice above Spitsbergen, attempted to surface through the ice at 81°59′N but failed, and returned to Norway where the vessel was later scuttled in Bergen Fjord.
1932	Soviet icebreaker *Alexander Sibiryakov*, with scientist Otto Schmidt as a passenger, to navigate the Northeast Passage, now called the Northern Sea Route, in one season	The ship, using power, sails, and finally being towed by a trawler from the Bering Strait, successfully completed the passage from west to east.
1933–1934	Otto Schmidt, in the Soviet ship *Chelyuskin* to travel the Northeast Passage again, and to resupply a camp on Wrangel Island	The *Chelyuskin*, a semi-icebreaker, sailed from Leningrad in 1933 but was crushed by ice early in 1934 and all hands were rescued by ice landings by Soviet aircraft.
1935	Will Rogers and Wiley Post, Americans	Both men were killed in an aircraft crash in the Alaskan arctic near Barrow.
1937–1938	Ivan Papanin, Soviet, to establish drifting ice station North Pole 1, at or near the North Pole	Papanin and party went by ship *Russanov* to world's most northerly island, Rudolph Island, at 82°N, then by four-engined aircraft to an ice landing at 89°58′N, seven miles from the Pole. After nine months of drifting, they were taken off the floe off the east coast of Greenland by the Soviet icebreaker *Taimyr*.

Approximate Dates:	Who and Why	Where, What, and Comments
1937–1940	Accidental drift of the Soviet icebreaker *Georgi Sedov* commanded by Badigin	Ship was caught in the ice in October, 1937, off the New Siberian Islands, and drifted to a point between Spitsbergen and Greenland where it was finally freed by another Soviet icebreaker in January, 1940.
1952	U.S. Air Force party, led by Lt. Col. J. O. Fletcher, to establish a drifting ice station on an ice island or tabular berg, accompanied by Capt. M. Brinegar and Dr. Kaare Rodahl	The party landed in March, 1952, and the ice island has since become known as Fletcher's Island or as T-3; it has been used periodically since that date, was the scene of a bizarre killing, and is still being tracked for future scientific use.
1958	USS *Nautilus* and USS *Skate*, nuclear-powered submarines	Both made submerged transits under the North Pole and across the Arctic Ocean.
1959	USS *Skate*, nuclear submarine, to surface through the ice at the North Pole	The submarine successfully surfaced at the Pole and, as a sentimental gesture, scattered the ashes of explorer Sir Hubert Wilkins there.
1967–1968	Ralph Plaisted, Minnesota businessman, for adventure and to publicize snowmobiles	Two attempts to reach the North Pole by snowmobile, the latter being successful
1968–1969	A dog-sledge expedition, British, led by Wally Herbert	Traveled from Alaska to the North Pole, then south to Greenland.
1969	United States tanker *Manhattan*	Completed the Northwest Passage.
1977	The Soviet icebreaker *Arktika*, using advanced Soviet ice-forecasting and icebreaking techniques, to the geographic North Pole	Traveling from Murmansk, via Novaya Zemlya and the Laptev Sea, the *Arktika* reached the Pole in August, 1977, returning to Murmansk via Franz Josef Land.
1978	Naomi Uemura, Japanese, alone by dog sledge, from Ellesmere Island to the North Pole	The early breakup of sea ice required his pickup by aircraft shortly after leaving the Pole. Uemura had taken a "training" trip earlier, alone, from Greenland to Alaska, by dog sledge, and, following his successful trip to the Pole, started and completed a sledging trip down the ice cap of Greenland, from north to south.

INDEX

219

Minerals *(continued)*
108, 135, 149. *See also* individual listings
Mongoloid people, 27
Mosquitoes, 54, 58, 120, 124
Muir, John, 62
Muktuk, 7
Murmansk, 58, 101, 102, 109
Musk ox, 120, 127, 133

Nansen, Fridtjof, 85
National Parks, 117, 176
National Science Foundation, 182, 184, 187
Native land claims, 11, 37, 59, 137, 149, 150, 151, 155, 158
Nautilus, 93
Naval Arctic Research Laboratory, (NARL), 9, 185
Navigation, 14, 16, 18, 72, 86
Nelson, Horatio, 79
Nickel, 100, 101
Nobile, Umberto, 89, 90
Nordenskjöld, Nils Adolf Eric, 85, 86, 184
Nordic Lapp Council, 144
Northeast Passage, 73, 84, 102
Northern Sea Route, 73, 84, 102, 178
North Pole
geographic or true, 2, 15, 16, 58, 69, 80, 84, 85, 86, 90, 91, 93, 181, 182, 186
magnetic, 12, 16, 18, 66, 80
North Slope Borough, 2
Norway, 4, 19, 50, 51, 59, 85, 98, 100, 102, 104, 108, 117, 129, 135, 139, 142, 144, 160, 182
Norwegian Sea, 50, 98
Northwest Alaska Native Association (NANA), 117, 128, 169
Northwest Passage, 73, 74, 76, 79, 80, 84, 85, 103, 106, 107
Northwest Territories, 58, 155, 174
Nuclear power, 65, 93, 103, 113, 149, 174, 185, 193
Nunavut, 158

Ob River, 51, 103
Oil, 4, 97, 98, 100, 106, 107–108, 109, 110, 125, 126, 150, 151, 160, 163, 171, 173, 181, 185, 191
Old Crow, 31–32
Onion Portage, 36
Ottawa, Canada, 4, 156
Otter, 127

Paleolithic, *see* Stone Age
Pangnirtung Pass, 61, 173

Papanin, Ivan, 90
Parry, William, 80
Partridge theory, 21
Peary, Robert E., 67, 85–87, 91
Pearyland, 58
Permafrost, 5, 45, 54, 57, 58, 102, 111, 165 ff.
Pesticides, 125
Pingoes, 58
Pipelines, 108, 158, 160, 167, 173, 181. *See also* Aleyska pipeline
Plaisted, Ralph, 91
Plankton, 122, 124, 126, 131, 173
Platinum, 100
Pleistocene, 27, 29, 125
Point Hope, Alaska, 8, 32, 34, 36, 170
Polar bears, 120, 121, 129, 137, 173, 176
Polar sector theory, 19
Population
Arctic Circle, 135
Alaskan Eskimo, 146
Canadian Inuit, 151
Greenlanders, 163
Grimsey, 60
Lapps, 142
Soviet Eskimo, 164
Spitsbergen, 100
Project Chariot, 149, 174
Prudhoe, Alaska, 58, 98, 106, 108, 109, 111, 150, 169
Ptolemy, 14
Pytheas, 70

Radiocarbon dating, 34–36, 62
Rae, John, 81, 83
Railroads, 108, 109
Rainey, Froelich, 32
Rasmussen, Knud, 32, 89
Ravens, 134
Reindeer, 113, 121, 128, 129, 142, 144, 145, 179
Religion, 9, 32, 40, 70, 131, 137, 139, 142, 143, 148, 158, 160
Resolute, Canada, 95, 99, 107, 119, 171
Rink, H. J., 161–162
Roads, 110, 111. *See also* individual highways
Ross, James Clark, 17, 80
Ross, John, 80, 99
Royal Canadian Mounted Police, 103, 155, 158
Runic stone, 72
Ruong, Israel, 145
Russia, *see* Soviet Union

Saber-toothed tigers, 28
St. Brendan, 70

About the Authors

Veteran author Cora Cheney has co-authored several books with her husband, Ben Partridge (Captain, USN, Ret.), who has dealt professionally with arctic matters for many years, most recently as an environmental law specialist. The peripatetic pair has lived and traveled in the arctic off and on for the last two decades. They have four grown children and live in South Windham, Vermont, when they are not off satisfying their curiosity about the world and its people.